Praise for **Heart Seeds**

"12,000 years ago the American continent was populated by native people crossing the Bering Strait. The wisdom they evolved guided their view of the world, their sense of interconnectedness, and their ways of making decisions. Today this wisdom, an oral tradition, is almost extinct. In *Heart Seeds*, WindEagle and RainbowHawk breathe immortality into this ancient wisdom. With an engaging, story-telling style they capture this ancient wisdom and provide the 'developed world' a unique opportunity to benefit from these time-tested perspectives on life and nature."
—*Eric E. Vogt, Co-founder and President, InterClass*

"Being raised in western civilization, *Heart Seeds, a Message From the Ancestors* helped me to understand on a deeper level why my energy is not balanced and why I often feel exhausted and stressed. The wisdom in the stories can unfold our potential for regaining individual wellness and becoming peaceful members in the global family."
—*Helga Breuninger, Breuninger Foundation, Germany*

"One needs only to read the headlines to see that our corporations and institutions and culture are suffering. As a people we are clearly at a time of great turning, and our response will define the fate of our world. If ever a people needed wisdom breathed into them, it is this day. *Heart Seeds* offers a deep collective wisdom, which is the medicine our ailing world so badly needs. WindEagle and RainbowHawk offer this gift outlining the path developed over many centuries to becoming a 'true human'—deeply connected to the community and focused on the well being of the whole. These lessons give us hope as we begin to remember and relearn how to live in relation to natural cycles, and are filled with the magic of life expressing itself."
—*Michael Thomas, Vice President HR & Corporate Social Responsibility, Granite Construction Inc.*

"In the aftermath of the annual International Day of Peace and being in conversation with organizations and Peacebuilders throughout the world, I can truthfully attest to the need for this gift to humanity—*Heart Seeds, a Message From the Ancestors*. There is a deep yearning for the wisdom of those who came before us to guide our pathways into the future and to remind us of the essential unity of Spirit that unites us amidst our diverse ways."
—*Avon Mattison, Founder and President, Pathways To Peace International Secretariat, "WE THE PEOPLES" INITIATIVE, a United-Nations-Designated Peace Messenger Initiative*

"One of the great religions of the world belonged to the Mayans, whose brilliant culture and insight vanished with the Spanish conquest of the American continent, but which lies hidden like a seed in the wisdom of the North American Indians. It is now springing forth again. This story is about an American couple with Native American roots who receive a revelation atop a Mayan pyramid, summoning them to awaken the seed of this ancient wisdom. The book is a fascinating and inspiring depiction of how this awakening is happening today."
—*Sven Damsholt, Wisdom Books, Denmark*

"There are many ways to walk into a circle, and many books out there about the ancient wisdom of indigenous American peoples. To those who want to learn more of this spirituality, *Heart Seeds* offers a new way to make that walk. The book opens the door to a sensitive, clearly laid-out step-by-step journey for the seeker. Woven through the book are many rich and beautiful historical stories and traditions, which the authors use to reveal these old teachings. They were never more vital and needed than today, when both our beautiful Mother Planet and the freedom of the individual are falling under deadly attack."
—*Patricia Nell Warren, bestselling author* One Is the Sun, The Wild Man *and other novels*

Heart Seeds

a message from the ancestors

WindEagle & RainbowHawk

EHAMA PRESS

HEART SEEDS, A MESSAGE FROM THE ANCESTORS
© copyright 2003 by WindEagle and RainbowHawk Kinney-Linton.
All rights reserved. No part of this book may be reproduced in any
form whatsoever, by photography or xerography or by any other
means, by broadcast or transmission, by translation into any kind of
language, nor by recording electronically or otherwise, without
permission in writing from the author, except by a reviewer, who may
quote brief passages in critical articles or reviews.

ISBN 978-1-7367408-0-4

Library of Congress Catalog Number: 2003114010

Typesetting and design by Mori Studio
Illustrations by RainbowHawk
Cover Illustration by Alowan Linton

Printed in the United States of America

First Printing: November 2003
Second Printing: January 2013
Third Printing: March 2021

17 16 15 14 13   5 4 3 2

EHAMA PRESS
P.O. Box 1205
Abiquiu NM 87510
https://www.ehama.org

It is our honor to dedicate this book to our grandchildren,
Christina, Rebecca, Patrick, Sarah, Hope, Maya,
and Torin, and to all the grandchildren everywhere.

Contents

Preface, ix
Acknowledgements, xiii
Editor's Note, xv

the Past

part One *The Gathering*
An Invitation, xxi

CHAPTER ONE—*Stories of the Old Way,* 1
The Departure, 1
The Medicine Singers' Invitation, 3
Learning From the Animals, 6
The Creation Story, 9
The Sacred Twenty Count, 13
The Story of Little Seed, 28
The Circle of Law, 32
Daily Life: Relationship With Mother Earth, 47

CHAPTER TWO—*Three Journeys to the Distant Past,* 54
Preparing for the Journey, 54
Journey to the Morning Star Kiva, 57
Journey to the Star Maiden Lodge, 69
Journey to the Council Longhouse, 79

part Two *The Journey of the Chiefs*

CHAPTER THREE—*The Dreaming Ceremony,* 93
  The Departure, 93
  The Far North, 96
  The Dreamer Chiefs' Welcome, 97
  Dreamtime Travel, 99
  The Women Chiefs Go Through the Obsidian Mirror, 102
  Reading the East Shield, 103
  Reading the South Shield, 104
  Reading the West Shield, 105
  Reading the North Shield, 107
  The Women Chiefs Return, 108
  The Mending of the Nets, 110

CHAPTER FOUR—*Looking Into the Shields of Humanity,* 111
  The Society of the East: Shield of the Spirit, 111
  The Society of the South: Shield of Emotion, 113
  The Society of the West: Shield of the Body, 116
  The Society of the North: Shield of the Heartmind, 118
  The Council Question, 120

CHAPTER FIVE—*The Transmission,* 123
  The Dreamer Chiefs, 123
  Awakening From the Dreamtime, 125
  The Wisdom Council, 127
  The Ceremony of Transmission, 130

the Present

part Three *Awakening and Remembering*

CHAPTER SIX—*The Call to the North,* 137
  The Heart Seeds Call, 137
  At the Conference in Mexico, 140
  At the Pyramid, 142

Going North, 145
Arrival and Greeting in the Land of the Dreamers, 148
Meeting With the Dreamer Chiefs, 154

CHAPTER SEVEN—*The Kiva Experience,* 160
  Entering the Kiva, 160
  The Nature of Reality, 162
  The Cycles of Human Growth, 166
  The Four-Day Medicine Singer Journey, 172
  The First Day—46,000 Years, 176
  The Second Day—5,000 Years, 180
  The Third Day—1,000 Years, 182
  The Fourth Day—100 Years, 185

CHAPTER EIGHT—*The Realization,* 190
  The Dreamer Chiefs' Words of Guidance, 190
  To the Island of the Dreamers, 191
  Reflections, 193
  The First Day of Ceremony, 195
  The Second Day of Ceremony, 213
  Feasting and Challenge, 220
  Preparation of the Rainbow Lodge, 223
  Ceremony of the Rainbow Lodge, 224
  Willow's Prayer, 230
  Recognition and Revelation, 231

the Future

part Four *A New Era*

CHAPTER NINE—*Parting the Veil,* 237
  A Year Later—The Vision, 237
  Looking Seven Generations Ahead, 239
  Opening the Dream of the Future, 240
  Reflections on the Dreamtime, 243
  The Animal Council, 245

Preface

The wisdom of human intelligence is an inherent part of our experience and heritage. Much of this wisdom has long been neglected and not seen as a vital part of our identity, particularly the intelligence of collective consciousness. In undertaking to write this book about ancient wisdom and aspects of vanished cultures of the past, we want to share with you, the reader, some of what has called us to write *Heart Seeds, a message from the ancestors.*

Long ago we were bidden by elders of the Native American Tradition to breathe these teachings into the world. "It is time," they said, "and maybe some good will come of it." That was the heart of the advice given us when we undertook the responsibility of being Medicine Teachers.

What is challenging about breathing the teachings into the world is that the wisdom of the old way arises from a culture of consciousness that is very different from today's world. We humans lived as tribal and clan societies for thousands and thousands of years, before what we now call "civilization" emerged. A deep wisdom, natural to humans, existed in this earth culture, and it was founded on and fostered the intelligence of collective consciousness.

The deepest part of this consciousness is recognized when we experience a sense of belonging, an identity that is larger than the separate and isolated self, the identity of being a real and viable part of the community, the tribe, or circle of the people. With the validation of this identity, there is an expansion of awareness of the individual's role in the wholeness of the group.

The earth cultures of indigenous peoples developed this awareness, this collective consciousness, into the high art of being the true human, unique and special individuals of spirit who contribute their gifts to the well being of the whole community. The stories of the people in this book will help the reader experience the kind of thought and protocols of awareness, which evolved from life lived in community, in intimate relationship with all aspects of nature and the teachings of Mother Earth. In our experience with people from all walks of life, observing their involvement in the teachings of the Medicine or Holy Way, we have seen that a deep hunger exists for humans to be reconnected to the wisdom of this ancient way of community.

The collective consciousness we refer to has been like a broad and deep river that has been flowing throughout the centuries. In the time of the earth peoples on our planet the river has been rich, fecund, abundant, wide, and deep. However, as our societies have changed and our connection to the earth became more distant, and our experience of living in community as a tribe or clan has changed, so has the river. At times it has become a small stream; in some places it has dried, with its flow stopped completely. And in some times it has been deeply hidden underground.

The stories of the Medicine Way, or the Holy Way, come to us through the earth, by way of an oral tradition passed from generation to generation. Some have held it close, and some have discarded it, while others have forgotten it. But always there have been those who carried the seeds of remembrance.

There have been many who have carried the old ways, names that are part of the journey song: Quetzalcoatl, Ocean Bow, Temple Doors, Flys Crow, Degahwenah, Tecumseh, Corn Planter and many others. And there have been many peoples all over this planet who have walked on the Earth Mother and who have carried the collective consciousness called the Beauty Way. On Turtle Island and Hummingbird Island some of the people were: Mayan, Tolec, Olmec, Hohokum, Anazazi, Hopi, Leni Lenapi, Iroquois, Ottawa, Mahegan, Cheyenne, and many many more.

It is our prayer in writing these stories of the people in the past, present, and future that you, the reader, will remember your own experience in the river of collective consciousness and help call it into being again. We know it is time for the river to be full, wide, deep, and once again providing abundance for all.

WindEagle & RainbowHawk
institute@ehama.org
www.ehama.org

Acknowledgements

We give our unending gratefulness to our editor and friend, Kate O'Keefe. Thank you, Kate, for your amazing questions, provoking the essence in us to come forward. Thanks for your loving inspiration, deep listening, and your outstanding abilities to multi-task! Mary, thank you for your wonderful laughter, early morning cups of coffee, and for always welcoming us with open arms.

Special thanks to our readers, Tom Schultz, Ken Marineau, Carol Manning, Jim Botkin, and Jeri Boisvert, who gifted us with excellent feedback and suggestions. Carol, your deep insights played a special part. Thank you all so much.

Our ongoing love and appreciation for G.M. "Jeri" Thornsberry, our administrative assistant. Thank you for your magical management of the "ten thousand things" there always seem to be.

Alowan, you captured such a magical feeling in your silk painting for the cover. You are such a gift. Thank you. Matthew, Olina, John, Sara, and Rob, thank you for your love and encouragement all this time.

And to Ted "D.R." Hughes, thank you for the beautiful holding of the land all these years. You give so much beauty from your hands and heart.

Fire Hawk, thank you for your amazing wizardry in creating and calling forth the magic of the "Animal Council" on a C.D.

Cole "E.E." Cameron, your gifts have been plentiful over the years. Special thanks to you for making it possible for us to do a major portion of our writing in Tulum. Our heart-felt thanks to you.

We send our deep appreciation to all our medicine family, in many places, who have listened to the stories around the fire. We send our love.

And finally to all of you who have ordered early or contributed to this first edition, our amazing and boundless appreciation.

And finally, we want to acknowledge a special and generous donation made . . .

In Memory of Michael P. Blondell
by
George and Karen McCown
The McCown Family Foundation
The Family of Michael P. Blondell

Editor's Note

Working with WindEagle and RainbowHawk on *Heart Seeds* has been a personal honor and a fascinating editorial challenge. Editors are trained to take out excess words and turn passive writing into active focused sentences. The Medicine Way of speaking, the way held by the ancient ancestors and by many tribal people today, is by its very nature passive. The passive voice is its authentic voice.

My challenge was to reduce the passive phrases and stipulations, which many modern English readers would find distracting or cumbersome, yet still retain the authentic voice of the storytellers. I trust this has been accomplished.

Those living or studying the Medicine Way will be familiar and at ease with the language. I hope those of you who are new to this "voice of the people" will be pleasantly challenged and that after some pages you will find yourself flowing with the poetic cadence of the language and slowing down to take in new perspectives.

I've learned a lot. The language we in the dominant culture call passive, I now call respectful, honoring, and complex. The value underlying this way of speaking is not on action taking, but on awareness, respect, and honoring. This language, I discovered, is highly relational, acknowledging and making explicit the oftentimes subtle connections that our everyday language assumes or, more likely, ignores.

I finally understood the intention of the language when, one day, I was editing a chapter and came to a phrase about the spider plant. The sentence said something about the plant and "the pot in which it grows." Quickly, I noted that the line be replaced with "its pot." Then, as I often did, I sat back and thought for a moment. I was constantly facing the choice between tightening up the language or letting it flow in the natural voice of the authors. Suddenly I understood that the first phrase intentionally acknowledges the relationship between the plant and the pot and by this acknowledgement honors the pot for its role in supporting the plant. By changing the phrase to "its pot," the pot became a thing, an object, and even something owned by or secondary to the plant.

The language in this book is not the familiar active voice of American English—full of pushing and possession. Rather, the language reflects the earth peoples' foundational beliefs—about balance, harmony, honoring, being true to one's heart, and being in relationship with the living universe that surrounds us.

I discovered that the passive voice is actually very active and extremely rich, complex, and nurturing. May you have a similar experience.

Kate O'Keefe

the Past

My friend,
They will return again.
All over the Earth,
They are returning again.
Ancient teachings of the Earth,
Ancient songs of the Earth,
They are returning again.
My friend, they are returning.
I give them to you,
And through them
You will understand,
You will see.
They are returning again
Upon the Earth.

Crazy Horse
Oglala Sioux (1842-1877)

part One
The Gathering

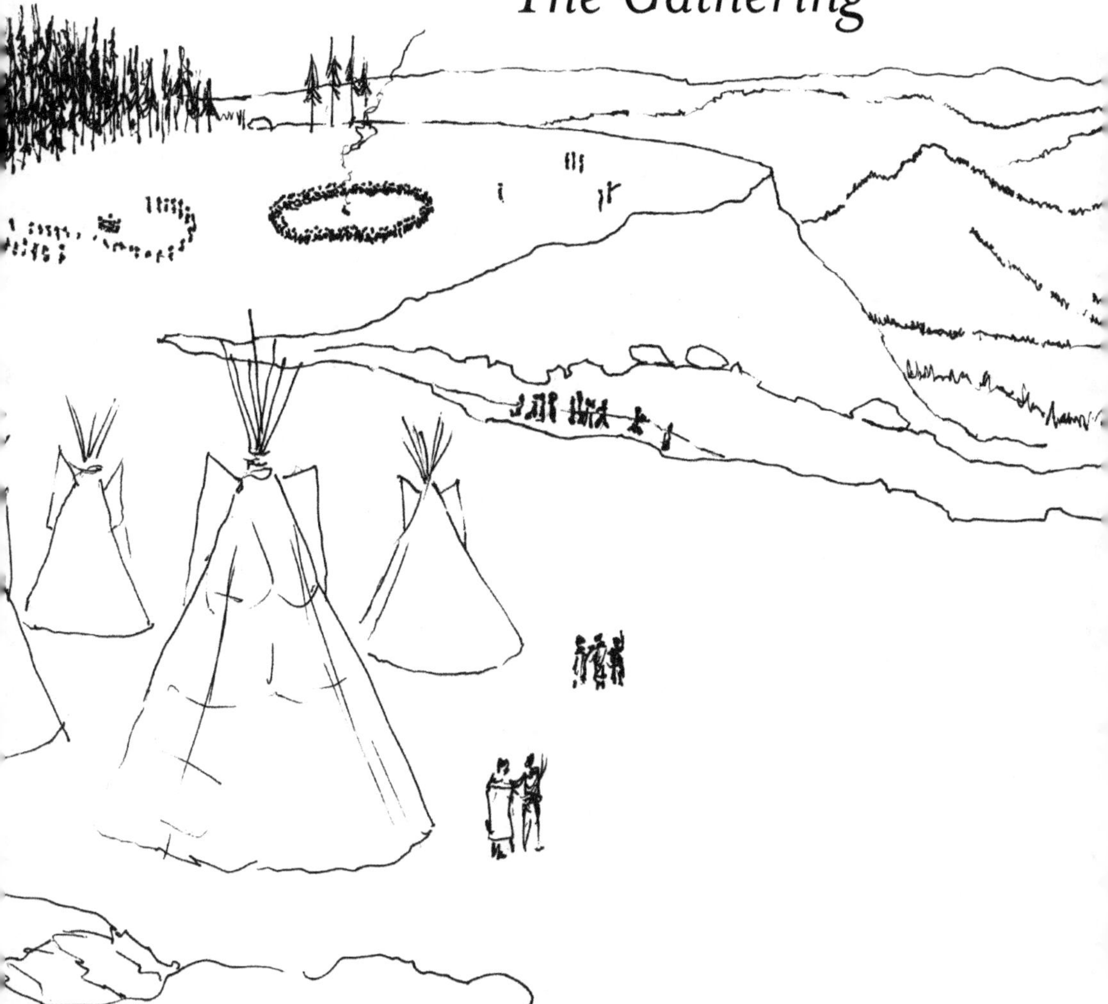

An Invitation

We ask the traveler beginning this journey of remembrance to imagine joining a gathering of representatives of the people that is taking place on Turtle Island (North America) some three hundred and seventy years ago (1634). This gathering has been called by the wise elders so that the people who will live in the future can remember deeply who they are and their ways of wisdom will not be forgotten.

For thousands of years the ancestors of these people have lived and moved about this beautiful land of the Mother Earth, living in clans and tribes. They evolved their customs and ways of life as they were affected by changes in weather, the flora and fauna of the earth, and by exchanges in culture affected by contact with other tribes, as the people migrated and interacted with one another.

Approximately one hundred years before this gathering that you, the traveler, are joining, the most recent influx of peoples from across the great ocean has taken place. The numbers of these newcomers have been increasing in the years before this gathering.

These new comers have begun their settlements in many places along the fringes of the land of Turtle Island, and with them they have brought a culture very different than that of the indigenous clans and tribes.

Already, at the time of this gathering of representatives of the people, there has been an impact of this very different culture. Many of the wise elders have seen a great change coming, which will affect the people's future more than anything they have in their memory.

So now, traveler, you are invited to be a part of this month-long gathering. The people's representatives will share their stories and ceremonies of celebration to help their people prepare for the future. You will hear some of these stories and go on some journeys of remembering with them. You can also imagine partaking in the camp life of hunting, feasting, play, and ceremonial ritual, which takes place during this gathering.

We wish you a rich time of remembrance and learning in this first part of your journey.

Chapter One
Stories of the Old Way

The Departure

The dawn light shifted the images on the skin of the lodge, making the shadows appear to be old ones approaching. Pathfinder, Medicine Singer for the tribe, was already moving with intention. He was among those chosen to attend the Great Gathering. He traveled with many men and women from his band, and the morning was filled with the usual bustling of so many preparing for the journey.

Tall and lean, strong muscled and dressed in leggings, with one small feather in his hair, Pathfinder looked, at first glance, to be a young warrior, such was his vitality. When the light caught his features, however, his skin, weathered and creased by the sun, revealed a man who had seen more than 60 winters. As Medicine Singer, rememberer, he carried a buffalo robe with markings from the last 43 winters on which he had painted the events which were remembered to be the most important happenings among the people.

His nephew, the youth he had chosen to accompany him, waited outside his lodge, ready with many bundles. As Pathfinder laid eyes on Little Wolf, he saw a boy of 13 summers who would soon be choosing his way in life. He was curious and thoughtful, qualities that would help him grow into a fine leader.

The people carried the things they needed for a long journey and a camp of one moon. They had over two moons of travel to reach the place of the Great Gathering. The people traveled light, however, knowing the earth would provide most of what they needed along the way.

Surrounded by low hills covered with oak and ash trees, the people walked through the valley. The greenish-yellow grasses, reaching higher than some of the young ones, almost hid them from view. As the sun made ready for its daily descent and the sounds of the life around them gradually quieted, the people finally reached the forest at the edge of the valley. Here they made their first camp, under the leafy green canopy with stars blazing overhead.

Days followed days as they crossed many rivers and slowly climbed higher and higher into the hills ahead.

The nights in the camps were peaceful, and many small fires were lit, while the people cooked what had been gathered along the way. Sometimes stories were shared. The travelers' anticipation grew as the weeks went by, and each of them sent out welcoming thoughts to those they would see before long.

The site of the Gathering was chosen for its accessibility to the many bands of people coming from different directions. It was to be held in a territory known to the people as the Wyoming, on the western flank of the Appalachian Range.

After many days of travel, the band led by Pathfinder joined together with the many other groups coming from all four directions of the land. This sacred place of the Wyoming had long been a gathering place for the tribes.

When celebrations and greetings were done and all representative groups had arrived, the people were called together.

The Medicine Singers' Invitation

We are the Medicine Singers, keepers of the memory of the people's stories, and we will guide you on this journey of remembrance of the past. Listening to the stories of our people is an old way of deepening our identity of who we humans are and helping us learn from and share with one another.

Our journey begins with the invitation. So let us walk to the top of that beautiful hill you see in the distance, covered with the tall standing ones, the pines. It is shady there, and a refreshing breeze brings the scent of remembrance to us as we walk. When we get there we will speak of the invitation.

Notice as we move how the long grass whispers to us as it slides past our legs. It seems to be saying, "Remember us, we are fresh new life, reborn of those who walked this land before." We are grateful for this gentle rhythmical reminder of the spirit of our ancestors who are with us this bright day.

Now, as we walk up the slope, see the sun-dipped needles of the standing ones! They beckon to us with their fingers of light, calling us to the Gathering at the top of the hill. It is a good day for gathering. Many others will be there. Together we will awaken our collective memory, for we have all been invited to this time, here on the Hill of Remembrance.

From this crest we can see a long way in every direction. See the river shimmering as it winds through the fields of grasses far below. Over there on the horizon see the sleeping ones, the Dreamer Peaks, figures of a man and woman lying side by side under the mountain sky. The figures are very old, from the beginning of time, dreaming above the endless forest below. Maybe they are dreaming us as we gather here.

This is a good place for us to talk. Let us all sit together in a circle on this old flat granite shelf. It is warm from the passage of Grandfather Sun and feels good on our backsides and legs after our long walk. To begin we'll pass the pipe around the circle and send a prayer of thanksgiving to the Old Ones. After you send your prayer, speak your name. That way we'll know who is here.

Ho! As the smoke prayers from the pipe rise into the sky, like our visible breath, we know our prayers have been heard. Thank you all for coming. Let us now introduce one of our elders from a tribe to the east, Pathfinder. He will speak now of this invitation, which has drawn us together on this hill.

The tall, slim, old man with weathered face and dark piercing eyes rises at the edge of the circle, his left hand raised to the sky.

"Recently, Wehomah, the Wind, spoke to our Elders in the voice of the evening breeze," spoke Pathfinder. "She told the Elders that it was time to gather the people for a journey of remembering. Stories of their learning and growing, which reveal who they were and how they lived, needed to be told. The stories are not just about the Elders; they are our story, as a people. Wehomah said it is important that the journey song of the people be made known.

"Our Elders understood that the message they received from Wehomah is important to us now. They have seen from this message that the current cycle of our people's journey is coming to a close. They have also seen that we will come again in a future time when our wisdom is needed. This time we now have together will strengthen the seeds that hold remembrance, so this knowledge can grow again when we return.

"The story is a good way for the mind of memory to hold the gems of the mystery," Pathfinder said. "These stories are a part of the great weaving of the people's journey. They belong to us and are carried in our collective memory.

"The challenge for each one of us, as representatives of the people during this time, is to listen deeply to these stories we share. It is important for us to call forth the strong images these stories will evoke, and by doing so we will make them a part of our collective memory of who we are as a people. During our time in ceremony we will enact elements of these stories in song and dance so they will be deeply imprinted in our memory. Also we will make paintings on skins, pottery, and weavings that we can take back to our different tribes to share the memories with our people. We will do these things to help our people, the men, women, and children of our tribes, to be strong in this time of change and so our ways will not be lost to the humans in the future.

"Now it is time for us to set up our lodges and make our camp and prepare our welcoming feast with thanks to the Great Spirit that has brought us here. We will begin our stories tomorrow with the morning sun."

At the completion of Pathfinder's speaking, the people rise and begin to move into the tasks of creating their camp. There is lighthearted banter among the people as some raise the lodge and some gather wood and build fires. The hunters go off to find game, and the women search for roots, herbs, and berries for the welcoming feast.

As this first day flows on and the camp takes shape, the people take time to renew old friendships and meet new acquaintances in a warm atmosphere of companionship and adventure. The good aroma of cooking food and campfires fills the air.

Later, after feasting, the drumming and songs begin, and the dancers move to the sacred beat, sending a message out that the people have gathered for an important ceremony. In the quiet of the night the full moon shines on the sleeping camp. Two wolves howl their plaintive song from a distant hilltop, and one of the camp dogs sends a sleepy growl before dozing off again.

Learning From the Animals

As the sun rises into the morning sky, the people gather again on the granite shelf, ready to share their stories. Across the circle a man, holding a young boy in his arms, stands and speaks.

"Thank you, Pathfinder, for your words of guidance and welcome yesterday. My name is Singing Waters and I will begin. What I have heard is that we have been called together here in this beautiful place to tell our story to each other. We all understand the power of memory in shaping our identity.

"We have lived a long time now as a people, and many tales of how we began and where we came from have shaped us, like the hands of the bowl-maker shaping the clay. This shaping has given us a sacred way that gives meaning to our life. I think we need to speak of these beginnings first, as we tell our story to one another. That was the first thing our elders taught us when we were young and sitting around the fire in our winter lodges.

"One of the tales that I remember hearing as a child was how we learned from the animals what it meant to be a human. I think hearing that tale again would be a good beginning.

"I see one of the elders here with us. I speak with respect, Grandmother Olin, and ask if you would tell that story to us now."

Our eyes follow the graceful movement of a gray-haired woman as she stands to speak.

"Ho, Grandson, it would be my honor," Grandmother Olin replied. "Many, many bundles of years ago, it was told the animal peoples gathered in council. It all happened because of Raven and Owl. You see, Raven had been on a long journey to the Great Sun and brought back the gift of fire. The story tells us he got too close, which is why he turned black. Anyway, when he returned he brought a message, which he told to Owl. The message from the Great Sun was that the animals must teach the new beings, called humans, how to live in this world, or they might accidentally destroy it due to their tendency to become self absorbed in their own importance.

"Owl, being the one who always asked questions and was therefore deemed wise, called out repeatedly to all the animals, night after night. This caused all the animals to come forward and gather in a great council. And after the council met, the animals began teaching their human relations how to listen, how to pay attention, and how to be alert like the animals. They also taught the humans how to find their way when they were lost, how to band together and care for one another, and how to read the signs of the plant people, the water people, and the star people. They taught these things and many others, but the most important was how to live with honor and respect for life and to give back.

"From these teachings the human beings learned how to be in a close relationship with all their relations, the Stars and Grandfather Sun, Grandmother Earth and her planet sisters and all her children—plants, animals, and humans. In time, the humans learned many things about themselves from these relationships. As long as the humans stayed close to their animal relations and were in respect of them, their wisdom grew and their way together became a way of beauty. In this way they knew abundance in the many lands on the Grandmother Earth.

"I have spoken," finished the grandmother.

"I am Shining Moon. Thank you for this remembering, Grandmother Olin. This story makes me think of my uncle Yellow Tail and when he asked me to go on a walk with him. It was just after I had heard the story of the animal council. I was young, and when he took me by the hand he seemed so big to me. I was in awe. He wore two eagle feathers in his braids, and as he talked they kept moving in the breeze, as if they were talking too.

"We walked to the edge of the village and into the forest. It was cool and shady there, very quiet and filled with mystery. I remember him pointing all around at the trees and sky, saying 'What the story of the animal council is saying to us, Little One, is that the trees and plants, the sky up there, and the earth under your moccasins are speaking things to you. These are things about yourself, inside yourself, that you must learn to listen to, about who you are and what meaning you carry in your life.'

"Just at that moment a deer leapt into the clearing, startling me. Uncle Yellow Tail squeezed my hand and made a sign for me to be quiet. The mother deer stood completely still and looked straight into my eyes. It seemed a long time, and then one ear twitched, like a wave, and she turned and was gone.

"Uncle Yellow Tail spoke after a moment. 'You see Little One? The animals know you are here. They have sent you a message. Mother deer is the bringer of truth. She has told you that you will grow into a strong woman, one who will always bring the truth of the heart to your people.'

"Then he said, 'That is what the story of the animal council teaches us. All of nature is of the Great Mystery—the waters, the sky, the rocks, the plants, the grasses, and the animals. They are all our true teachers, speaking to us constantly. They speak in the language of mystery, telling us humans who we are and our meaning in life, for we are made from them and are one of their voices. You must learn to listen well, Little One.'

"The time spent with my uncle set me on a path of listening and awareness. I have always tried to remember his words. I have spoken."

The people are stimulated, hearing these first stories and, is often the custom, small groups of representatives cluster together to share thoughts that come to them as they listen. Many share incidents of their learning with their elders when they were young, and a number of children gather around the small groups, listening with wide eyes.

The Creation Story

After a time one of the men stands and signals, holding his palm up. Quickly the groups quiet to hear him speak.

"I am Little Bear. Ho, Shining Moon, the words of your story are good and true. You have brought your heart of truth to our councils many times over the years, even when sometimes it was painful for us to hear. It is good to hear the story that tells of a beginning time in your life. As I have been talking with some of my friends I have been reminded that part of our story as a people is of another beginning. It is one we need to hear to truly remember our origins. I see the Dreamer Chiefs from the North sitting across this large circle. I will ask them if they will tell the story of The Dance," completed Little Bear.

We all watch as the Old Man and the Old Woman are approached by a young man sent by Little Bear. They each listen and think for a moment and then, eyes sparkling, nod to each other. They tell the young man they will comply with Little Bear's request. Seats are prepared for them as they make their way to the center of the circle.

The Old Man speaks first. He says that the story of The Dance is one of the many creation stories of the People and reminds them that wisdom and knowing come through the images. He says it is best for us to allow the story to come alive in our own vision. Then he steps back, softly chanting, and begins making a heart-beat rhythm on his drum.

The Old Woman begins. She speaks slowly, as the wind carries each of her words directly into our hearts. The graceful movements of her hands paint moving images while her voice transports us into the story.

"In the beginning was the Great Great Grandmother Wakan, the Void—stillness, all potential. She was complete and whole in every way, and she was lonely. And in Her loneliness She turned in upon Herself, and Ssquan, the Great Great Grandfather—the Lightning Bolt, the kinetic life force—came into being.

"The Great Great Grandmother Wakan and the Great Great Grandfather Ssquan came together and knew one another and from this dance came their first born—Grandfather Sun, all Stars.

"Once again the Great Great Grandmother Wakan and the Great Great Grandfather Ssquan danced together and knew each other, and from this union came their second born—Grandmother Earth, all Planets. So it was in the beginning, so it is now, and so it will be.

"Ho, and I say, Grandmother Earth and Grandfather Sun danced, and from this came their first born—the Plants.

"And Grandmother Earth and Grandfather Sun once more danced their dance and knew each other, and their second born came into being—the Animals.

"Ho, and I say, Grandmother Earth and Grandfather Sun came together, danced, and through their union came their third born, the Human. So it was then, so it is now, and so it will be. I have spoken."

We sit in silence for a few timeless moments after the Old Woman completed her story. The Old Man makes room for her to sit down beside him. When he starts to speak the Old Woman begins shaking her rattle softly, and his words begin to flow.

"When I first heard my grandmother tell the story of The Dance, I was still quite young. And each time I have heard it, the story has revealed something new. At first I giggled as I imaged the Sun and the Earth dancing and having plant children and animal children and even human children. That was hard to understand. But I thought about it many times, and as I grew older many things came clear to me. Now that I am an old man, I'll share what I have learned.

"My learning really started when all the young men were taken out for training and initiation, to prepare us to step into the tribe for the first time as men. We had some very powerful teaching in those months. I remember my grandfather, War Horse. He was the war chief for our people and our first teacher in that time.

"He taught us that the Great Great Grandmother is the feminine aspect of the Great Spirit and that we find her in the silence of the night and in the build-up before the storm. She is the void which is the fullness of all potential, all that can become manifest. He said we each have her feminine energy inside us, even a great war chief like War Horse, and that we must always draw on her power before we act.

"He also taught us that when we take action or create we are calling on the energy of the Great Great Grandfather, the masculine energy of the Great Spirit, and that we carry this energy inside of us too.

"I have come to know this as the *being* and the *becoming*, the twin energies of life, the yielding and the changing. I know now that these energies of The Dance are in all things and that The Dance continues every moment of every day. Maybe the most important part of this understanding for me was to see this great potential in every person and in every situation. I found that knowing this has changed the way I see things and what I expect from life. I now know that anything is possible.

"Well, I am an old man, and I have maybe talked too long. I will be quiet now. I have spoken."

The old Dreamer Chiefs return to their seats, and at that moment the drummers begin a rousing beat. A dance leader, wearing a headdress of wild turkey feathers and carrying a long staff, moves into the circle. With piercing whoops he calls the people to move into dance with him, celebrating and enacting the visions the stories have evoked.

Soon the granite shelf is alive with the movement of the people, some moving like the animals of the stories, some in shuffling patterns like star formations, and others in creative expressions of what was heard in the stories. Each dancer is intent on their own vision as they dance the images into the memory of their body.

Later the dancing is complete, food is shared, and different groups form to paint on skins and weave designs of what the stories held for them. These they will take back to their people. This was a time of rich sharing in community, remembering the long journey song and events that made up the fabric of their lives as a people.

There is no sense of hurry in the people, for each knows they must take the time needed to let the meaning of the stories sink deep into their memory, like the rain filtering down to the roots of the tree to bring nourishment. With this sense of community and ceremony the daily life of the camp continues. The people tell more stories, play with one another, perform creative activities, contemplate in silence, and sing and dance to the drums. Some paint or weave images, and many help hunt and gather food. Meals are prepared and shared, and rich conversations are had around the evening camp fires.

The Sacred Twenty Count

Five days of the ceremony have passed, and the camp is still engaged in practices and rituals of deepening their appreciation and memory of their way of relationship with the mystery of creation and all their relations. On this sixth morning, the whole camp gathers at the request of Pathfinder to continue sharing stories about their learning as a people. A stalwart, broad-shouldered man of middle age, wearing fringed leather garb and holding a hunter's bow, stands and speaks.

"I am Standing Tree, and it is good to hear these things again as we talk together about our way and how we have become who we are, the people. I speak words of gratitude to our Dreamer Chiefs for their telling of the old creation story and how it speaks of the power of the feminine and the masculine, the forces of being and becoming that are in all things.

"I call to mind now, in our time together, how we were all taught as youngsters, and that this was called the Children's Count, or the beginning of the sacred numbers. As we began our learning we would hold up one finger and chant, 'One is the sun;' then two fingers up, 'Two is the earth,' we chanted; then three fingers, 'Three the plants;' then four fingers, 'Four the animals.'

Last, we would raise our hands, all five fingers stretched out, and shout 'Five the humans!' Then we'd point at each other and roll on the ground laughing.

"But the story stuck with us like an arrow in a tree. Our young teachers would have us go around many days pointing at Grandfather Sun in different places in the sky saying 'One is the Sun;' then again with Grandmother Earth, and once more with all the plant beings we could see. We spent another day with animals that we could creep up on. I remember River Boy and myself stampeding the horses when we sprang out of the bushes, screaming 'Four, the Animals!' Our fathers did not appreciate that. But the funniest time was when we spent several days leaping out, pointing at our relatives, and shouting, 'Five, the Human!' We would bend over laughing when they jumped in surprise.

"We didn't realize then that a ground of recognition was being set for our understanding of the Sacred Twenty Count, which is the foundation of our Way of the Council. Thus, we had deeply planted the seeds of relationship and recognition of these forces in our lives.

"I was 13 the first time I heard the Sacred Twenty Count. It was shortly after my rite of passage to become recognized as an adult being, and I was very proud and full of myself. On a hot spring morning I was in a wood grove practicing shooting targets with my twin sister Sacisha. She had notched a better score that I had, and I was annoyed. Suddenly through the trees came Cetin, the elder, trailed by 40 or so of our camp's young men and women.

"Cetin stopped and looked at Sacisha, our targets, and me. Then he said, 'Bring your bow and arrows, both of you. We'll go learn something important that will help you to put a leash on your ignorance. It might even help you to know how to hit a target when you intend to, maybe even as good as your sister, so you don't have to frown so much.'

"So we picked up our arrows and unstrung our bows and followed the group. Cetin led us out of the grove and into a large clearing with sandy ground. He had everyone stand to one side of the clearing while he took his staff and drew a large circle in the sand, about 15 paces across. Then he looked in the direction where the sun rose in the morning and made a mark at the edge of the circle. Then he walked across the circle and made a mark opposite the first one.

"'That first one is East' he said, 'in the direction where the Grandfather Sun rises. That's a good place to start most things.'

"Then he said, 'Where I'm standing now, opposite the East, is the West. North and South are to my left and right at the edge of the circle.' He walked to each of these and marked them. Then he went around the circle and made four more marks, dividing each quarter in half.

"'These are called the marriage points,' he continued, pointing to the last four marks. Swinging his staff in an arc around the circle and pointing to each mark in turn, he said, 'This circle represents the universe, and these marks are the eight gateways of knowledge. We humans are here to learn and grow. That is our spirit journey.'

"Cetin looked at each of us in turn. Standing close to us he spoke in a soft voice. 'We human beings have the tendency to be ignorant. It is our greatest challenge. Ignorance is when we turn away from what we can't see or can't understand. Things we can't see well or understand confuse us or even frighten us,' he said, 'and we don't like being confused or frightened. And that is when we begin to ignore.'

"Then Cetin laughed and began a little hopping dance, twirling his staff over his head and shouting, 'But I am going to trick you out of your slothful ways of ignoring so you can become humans instead of two leggeds! I am going to plant a seed of a design in your mind that will grow the flowers of the knowledge of remembrance. You will spend the rest of this life needing to tend this garden of relationship. And if you nourish it, and pull out the weeds of distraction, you may yet become humans and be of use to your people.'

"Next Cetin looked directly at me and with a smile he said, 'If you allow this design to take root in you, you may be able to see someday that there is no separation between you, your arrow, and the target you aim for. When you see that you will become a true hunter.'

"Cetin continued his teaching, saying 'Now I will introduce you to the Sacred Twenty Count, the ancient way of seeing into the Mystery of Life. It is an ancient design, which reflects all the energies of the universe. All energy has consciousness. The Mystery is energy consciousness. It is everywhere and in everything. The Mystery is that which we can see and that which is unseen.'

"With these words spoken, Cetin picked ten of the young women of the group and gave each one a number from 2 through 20. He then picked ten of the young men and gave us numbers from 1 through 10. My number was 5. He had all of us gather around the outside of the circle he had drawn in the sand.

"Next, Cetin walked into the center of the circle and drew a diamond in the sand with his staff. It was about

Chapter One—Stories of the Old Way

Sacred 20 Count

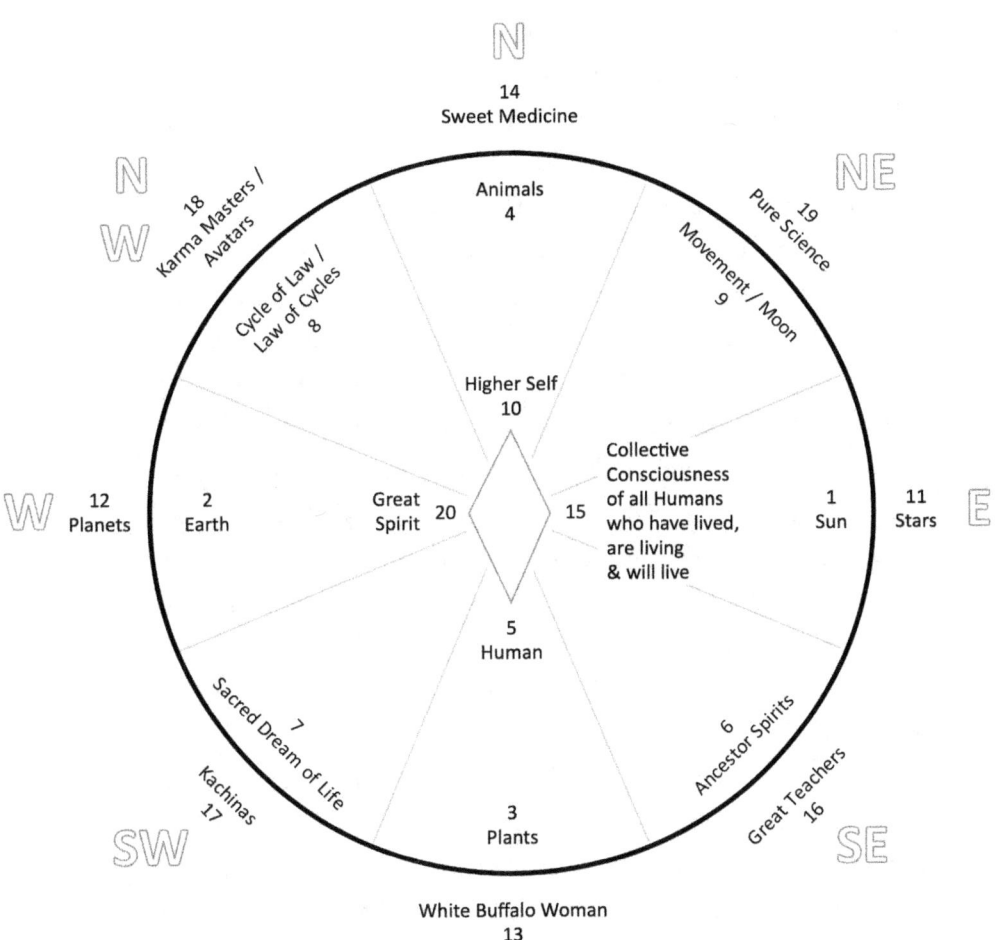

three paces in length on the North–South axis and about two paces in width on the East–West axis. 'Here is a symbol in the center of the circle of the universe, the diamond of the Sacred Self of the human,' he said. 'This symbol represents each one of you, and me, too; and each member of our tribe, your mothers and fathers, your sisters and brothers, and all your human relatives and friends, even those you don't consider to be friends. This is a design of human consciousness to help us to remember all of our relationships—relationships with all the energy consciousness of the universe.'

"'By the way,' Cetin said, smiling, 'I'm not sure if the animals or plants have a design like this to help them, but if they did I'm sure they would be in the center, not us.'

"I remember we all thought this was terribly funny, and some were saying, 'Yes, what about a horse wheel?' 'What about a turkey wheel?' And one girl said 'Yeah, how about a worm wheel!' And then we all broke up, laughing and shoving each other around.

"'All right! All right!' shouted Cetin. 'You're all here to learn something, so pay attention.' Cetin, when he wanted to, could burn holes in you with his eyes, so we all got quiet again.

"'Standing Tree,' Cetin called, 'you have the number 5, so you come here and stand at the south point of this diamond. You represent the human here, so see if you can act like one for a few minutes and not a two-legged funny man.' I know I got red in my embarrassment, but I stepped forward smartly to attention and took my place at the south of the diamond.

"Then Cetin called the number 10 and pointed to the north of the diamond, and one of the boys stepped forward and took that spot. Then 15 and 20 were called, and two girls ran in and stood at the east and west points respectively. There we were, four of us standing in the middle of our circle of peers, trying to look impressive, while Cetin circled around our diamond like a wolf on the hunt.

"'You are representing the consciousness of the human,' he stated, as he looked at each of us in turn. 'In the south of the diamond is the sacred number 5, the human; in the north, 10, the higher self; in the east, 15, collective consciousness of all humans that have lived, are living, or will live.'

"Cetin had us all repeat this one several times till we got it right. Then Cetin moved to the girl at the west point of the diamond and touched the top of her head with his staff and said, '20, Great Spirit.'

"Moving around the outside of the big circle where the rest were standing, Cetin paused and then continued. 'So, you see, our ancestor chiefs understood that each human was made up of four levels of consciousness. Our human manifestation level, our higher consciousness level that connects us to all energy, our collective consciousness level that relates us to all human experience, past, present, and future, and finally the Great Spirit level that connects our world to Wakan-Ssquann, Great Great Grandmother and Great Great Grandfather. Any questions yet?' asked Cetin with a challenging wolf smile, looking as if he would pounce at any moment.

"We were all shuffling from one foot to the other, some of us looking at the sky, like maybe a good question would appear there. Others were studying their feet, hoping that maybe the Mother Earth would send some intelligent response up from the sand we were standing on. Silence.

"Then suddenly my sister Sacisha, showing her winning smile, spoke.

"'Honored Elder,' she said, 'I am one of us that hasn't been given a number for this game today, but I heard you say that this diamond of numbers represents each one of us, and that includes me and my human consciousness. My question is, where do I imagine myself standing in this image you are painting for us?'

"At that moment I remember I felt relieved that Sacisha had broken open the wall of blackness that we were all enclosed in, releasing us from the whip of Cetin's tongue. At the same time I must admit that my young male pride was tweaked by jealousy since she had come through first again. But Cetin's response brought me quickly back to the moment. He jumped into the air, twirling a full circle, landing gracefully on both feet, and then springing across the circle to Sacisha's side, shouting, 'Quick, quick! Come with me before the import of this question is lost in the surrounding sea of unconsciousness!'

"Cetin led Sacisha in a dash to the center of the diamond where they stood surrounded by four of us holding the 5, 10, 15, and 20. 'This is where each of you must imagine your center place,' he said. 'This is the home of your Sacred Self, surrounded by your four levels of human consciousness. As you move through the journey of your life, if you remember to come from this center place you will always know your true spirit power, and you'll walk in a relationship of command, with the energies of life touching you and emanating from you. That is why you must learn to hold your teachings and these designs forward in your memory mind, so you can always find your way home to yourself.'

"We all felt a wave of excitement at getting this beginning glimpse of ourselves moving with a sense of power and command in what our parents and teachers had many times referred to as our 'self authority' and 'self responsibility.' It was beginning to make sense, like the first scent the bear has when seeking the honey. But we had a lot yet to learn, and Cetin didn't let us forget it.

"'Now I'm going to introduce you young fish to the deep waters in which you will learn, in time, to swim with ease,' spoke the elder, Cetin. 'Know this: that we humans live in an ocean of energies we call the Life Mystery, and this energy consciousness is speaking to us in every moment. You must learn to listen to these energies for they will teach you what part you play in the dance of life and death and how to play it. This is a cycle of creation that never ends. This circle, which we are standing around, represents the entirety of this ocean of mystery, this universe, this one sacred song of life.'

"'So that you can hear the different notes in this ocean of energies, I am going to call your remaining numbers to the eight different gateways of knowledge I have marked around the perimeter of this circle,' Cetin said. Pointing his staff towards each of the marks he had made at the beginning, he said, 'Don't forget, you are in the center—here—swimming in these waters.'

"Then Cetin began calling the remaining numbers in pairs, '1 and 11 at the East gate.' And a young man and a young woman stepped into the circle at the East. Pointing at the young man, Cetin said, 'You hold the sacred number 1, and you represent the Sun.' Then Cetin had us all repeat, '1 is the sun.' Then he pointed at the young woman. 'You hold the sacred number 11 and you represent the stars.' And we all repeated, '11, the Stars.'

"'Now here is something to remember in this design,' said Cetin. 'All the young women have the numbers above 10. Each of these numbers represents the collective energy consciousness of all the manifestations of the numbers 10 and above. For example, the Sun is a singular manifestation, while 11, the Stars, is the collective energy consciousness of all stars. This will be true of the numbers at each gateway. This collective energy force field has a lot to do with how we experience the world.'

"I know that for me a lot was flashing through my thoughts, and I could sense all my brother and sister fish were trying to keep oriented in this deep water, too. But Elder Cetin sensed this and made the calming sign with his palms down parallel to the Mother Earth, his staff leaning to the curve of his neck and shoulder.

"'Steady now,' he said. 'Remember I told you this was deep water. I think I have a sense of what you're feeling. I recall my first time hearing these things, and I was both excited by a feeling of recognition and at the same time wondering how I would remember it all. I felt a little like a wolf cub out on the first hunt with its mother, all eagerness and bumbling about at the same time. But it's like anything else new you have learned, like your first time swimming; you were excited, but concerned about staying afloat.'

"'What I want to have you experience,' Cetin went on, 'is your first seeing of this subtle design our ancestors passed on to us and a few words about its meaning and how to begin working with it. In time it will work smoothly in you. It will talk to you and teach you how to relate deeply with the life in you and around you. In time it will teach you how to be a chief in our councils and how to add your wisdom to the pool of the people's wisdom.'

"'Right now we're going to identify each of these sacred numbers in their place around this circle of remembrance. We are going to do this quickly, and then I'll say some words of explanation and suggestions for your practice. Here we go:

- In the West—2 and 12—Earth and Planets.
- In the South—3 and 13—Plants and White Buffalo Woman.
- In the North—4 and 14—Animals and Sweet Medicine.

Now the marriage points.

- In the Southeast—6 and 16—Ancestor Spirits and Great Teachers.
- In the Southwest—7 and 17—Sacred Dream of Life and Kachinas.
- In the Northwest—8 and 18—Cycle of Law/Law of Cycles and Karma Masters/Avatars.
- In the Northeast—9 and 19—Movement/Moon and Pure Science.'

"'Look around you now,' Cetin said, 'and see this symbolic design of the energies of the universe that you have enacted with your bodies. You are standing in the Sacred Twenty Count with the number of the Sacred Self at the center.'

"At that moment something moved in me that I have never forgotten. As I looked around at my brothers and sisters standing in pairs at each of the gateways, I saw many colors and textures. I saw them carrying lances with bright pennants and eagle feathers moving in the breeze. On their heads they each were wearing beautiful plumed helmets that sparkled and shimmered with a radiance like sunlight reflecting on the afternoon lake. It was as if I was standing in the midst of the universe, surrounded by all the energies of life represented by these noble figures, and all of them were speaking to me in turn. Like a great drum their wisdom was pulsing through me, transforming me into a beautiful song that spread out in expanding circles of sound. It was a moment of my youth that I have always carried with me as part of my journey song.

"Cetin called us to attention after a few moments of silence, and went on to make a few concluding comments. He walked to each gateway and spoke several arrows of thought about what each of the sacred energies was and how they moved in the life around us and in each one of us. I recall that first time how I was filled with wonder as even the ones I thought I knew were opened wider in awareness within me. He taught that the plants are the transforming energy and that in their magic they change the earth into the living substance that becomes food to eat and air to breathe.

"Many of the higher numbers that represent the more subtle collective energies of life manifestation were stirred in remembrance within me by Cetin's poetic eloquence. He told us that we must keep holding this remembrance of relationship in our consciousness always, and that in time each of them would reveal their deeper and deeper significance to us about who we are and our part in the Life Mystery.

"Elder Cetin surprised us again by announcing that we were all going to spend the next four days and nights

right there in that circle, having a ceremony of remembrance together. Then he sent us out to gather birch branches to build two lodges, one for the young women in the west of the circle and one for the young men in the east of the circle. And he had us build a fire in a pit we made in the center of the circle.

"About that time a number of the elders emerged from the forest bearing blankets and boughs for our sleeping needs. Others brought water and special herb teas. Full of smiles and jokes, they waved and went into the forest again, singing an old honoring song. It was good to know that we were all held by the village at this time; that helped us to settle down from the surprise Cetin had given us.

"In those four days and four nights Cetin had us gather stones to place around the wheel. He gave us eight banners to mount on lodge poles, which we staked at each of the eight gates. Then he drilled us on the Twenty Count and taught us how to speak as if each energy was speaking through us. He made clear that we each would have to fashion a much larger image lodge of what our Self was, in order to hold the greater relationship.

"'The little 'I' that you call yourself now is only a small part of the larger mystery that each of you are. As you acquire more knowledge about your Self lodge, it will grow larger. And when it is big enough,' he said, 'you will be called upon to be a chief in the peoples' councils, for this sacred Twenty Count is the foundation wheel of our wisdom way.'

"I am Standing Tree and I have spoken."

At this moment a tall slender woman with gray hair touching her temples stands across the circle from Standing Tree, sending him a loving smile. She is Standing Tree's sister.

"Ho! I am Sacisha, and you have told this story well, Standing Tree. For a long time now you have been a great hunter. And I see that you are a great hunter with words too, bringing to our feast these images of remembrance. Many years have passed, but I still see that first youth wheel with young eyes. We were so proud of the beauty we created. Our eyes were damp with the waters of joy when the elders came that day and blessed the wheel with sage and song and dedicated it to all future youth. It still exists, you know. As I rode by that village on my way here, I saw a circle of young ones in the wheel. The trees we planted are tall now, and their long leafy branches give continual shade. And all the flowers and grass are so beautiful to see!

"Thank you, my dear brother, for taking us back to that time," said Sacisha, smiling.

Each of us is touched deeply as we listen to this amazing story, somehow feeling we have been a part of that early time. We talk among ourselves for a while, some remembering their own journey of learning and some simply lying on the earth, watching the clouds in the sky. Then, after a time of reflection, the big drum sounds, and Pathfinder calls all of the representatives together again.

"It is appropriate at this point in our ceremonial gathering," Pathfinder begins, "for each of us to renew our relationship to this teaching of the Sacred Twenty Count. To do this we call all of us to participate in building such a sacred space as described in Standing Tree's story. We will need to do this in the large meadow over there behind the trees at the back of our granite shelf. Each time we create such a wheel on the Mother Earth, she knows we have made a way for us to listen to Her and the Great Mystery she is a part of. Also, it will be good for our young ones here, to deepen their understanding of this teaching."

Pathfinder completes this suggestion, and the representatives organize themselves in various groups to accomplish the tasks needed to create a beautiful medicine wheel. Some set about to gather stones for the perime-

ter, some to shape flag poles and others to create flag pennants. Over the next five days the camp engages in this activity and dedicates this space in the meadow to Mother Earth with songs and dances, prayers and speeches. At each step there are those who teach the young, instructing them as they help create the wheel. During these days of celebration all the usual daily activities of camp life continue. Several purification sweat lodges are also built, and each day groups partake in these renewal rituals.

The Story of Little Seed

On this the thirteenth day of the gathering, the representatives once again come to the granite shelf to continue sharing the stories of their teaching way. The people settle to listen, and a young woman with two children at her side calls everyone to attention.

"I am Listening Crow, and I have a question. I am grateful for the words of the elders and hope that I can someday become a powerful rememberer. In this time I deeply need to remember about living in harmony. May I ask to hear the story of the harmony of the people? What made it possible for our people to live together in balance with each other for so long?"

Many nod as we wait to see who will stand and reply to this question. We watch an elder grandmother begin to rise. She stands, with the help of those around her. The sun brightens the silver tones of her hair and seems to outline her tan-colored shawl.

"Ho, I am SeedPlanter, elder from the east. It is a good question you have asked, Listening Crow, and I will begin the remembrance story.

"My story begins on a cloudy day when I was about 11 summers. I was journeying with my grandmother, Singing Rain, who was a great woman chief. I was a little afraid to be alone with her on our long journey because she was a strict teacher, and I knew how much my time with my grandmother meant to my mother, Badger. My mother had sent me on this journey to learn.

"I was truly suffering that day. Being the oldest girl, I had been helping my mother create a new tipi, and I had not been riding much lately. Now, with eight hours riding the day before and seven on that day, my muscles were beginning to cramp and I was worried about staying on my horse. I was afraid I might not be able to keep up with my grandmother's pace. And that was not all; I had been worrying about my time of ceremony that was to happen in four moons. I was wondering about what society I would enter. I knew I had to speak of this soon, but I feared that what I wanted might not be accepted by my mother and my grandmother.

"That night, after we had made camp and had eaten a small bit of food, my grandmother was peering at me across the fire with her eagle eyes. She knew something was brewing in me, and she was waiting to see if I would have the courage to speak.

"'Well, Little Seed, what have you got stuck in your beak?' she asked.

"I didn't earn the name SeedPlanter until much later in my life. I lowered my eyes and replied, 'Nothing grandmother.' It was then that she told me the story of Little Seed.

"'One day Old Planter was working in the soil singing to the seeds of how they would grow into tall strong plants that would giveaway to the people. He sang his gratitude while he worked, and because he cared for the plants and the earth so much and had such love in his heart, he became very sensitive. Old Planter could hear the plants talking.'

"'The sun was hot that day and he had been working hard, so in the middle of the day he sat under a tree to rest and drink some water. He closed his eyes and listened to the song of the birds. And that's when he heard Little Seed. She was crying. She had been hiding in his planting basket because she was terrified to go into the ground. The ground was dark, and she was afraid she would be lost. But most of her sisters and brothers had already left and she was feeling terribly lonely in the basket. So very quietly, Old Planter began to sing to her. In the song he told her she would be with her true mother, the Earth, and that when her seed opened her roots would come forth into a wonderful new experience of freedom. And it would be at that time that she would connect with her brothers and sisters, and they would remember her. Even now, he sang, they were searching for her roots to touch theirs. Once that happened she would begin to grow into her true beauty. Little Seed had stopped crying some time ago, as she listened to Old Planter's song. Her heart didn't hurt anymore and she had begun to feel something brand new for her.'

"After the story I noticed the silence and saw Grandmother looking at me across the fire. She asked what I thought Little Seed was feeling. I didn't have to think very long because I was feeling the same thing—excitement! Now I knew I had to speak to my grandmother and my mother about what was inside of me. If I didn't I would be lost in the dark all by myself. I found I had new courage and wanted to open up. Expressing myself and growing into a young woman was more important than anything else.

"For me this was a turning point in my young life, and I have not forgotten the many teachings on that long journey with my grandmother. I continue to appreciate her wisdom. In this one story she taught me how important it is to speak and not to keep things inside.

"This is the true right of each human. We must have this freedom as a people, and the first place we must find it is inside ourselves. True freedom comes when we express our spirit. Without freedom of expression we cannot experience harmony as a people. Instead we find ourselves hiding our true feelings and thoughts. This creates separation and mistrust. Freedom of expression is the beginning of harmony in the Self and in the people.

"She also taught me how to see the people as a connected whole, a part of the Earth Mother and how we can support each other as we learn and grow. This is the second aspect of harmony.

"Later on that journey my grandmother told me about the Sacred Dream, which is like a seed in each of us. She said we have to plant and tend that seed in order for it to grow.

"'We are each like Little Seed,' she said. 'Our destiny is to grow into our true beauty and offering the fruits of that uniqueness is our giveaway.' The manifesting of our Sacred Dream is the third element in creating harmony as a people.

"So now I have sung my song of remembering to you. May it be like a seed inside your heart where true harmony grows. And I sing out my song of gratitude to you Singing Rain, my grandmother. I remember you. I am SeedPlanter, and I have spoken."

The Circle of Law

SeedPlanter finds her seat, and someone stirs across the circle. We all know Leaping Dolphin from his colorful tales, and our hearts begin a new rhythm in anticipation of his words. Today he looks his age, an elder of 85 years, yet vital. The piercing energy of his blue eyes flashes across our faces. We lean in to catch every word as he begins.

"Ho, I am Leaping Dolphin, Elder of the South. I have heard your words, SeedPlanter, and as all good gardeners, you have tilled the soil well with your stories. When I listen to the seeds of harmony planted by your grandmother's words, I hear my own father speaking to me of the Circle of Law. As long as I have known you, SeedPlanter, since you were 15 summers, you have carried your wisdom in a quiet and subtle way. And this is good. It is good because we need to be able to find our own path of knowing and by finding our own way, we claim our learning for ourselves. So this quiet way is good, but now I want to shout!

"I will tell about the Circle of Law from a warrior's view. I have been a war chief for more years than I can count, and I want to tell you about my first battle with the enemy. I will tell a story that will bring you to the Circle of Law, so just sit back and let me take you there. Indulge this old man.

"I was quite arrogant as a youth," Dolphin said, looking around at the others. "Some of you smile as you can still see the threads of that quality now, even at 85 summers. But that boy of 13 summers, he was quite big headed.

"The way I remember it, I was pretty puffed up about winning a running race. In fact I was practically sprouting peacock feathers. A group of us had spent the summer testing our skills, shooting targets, trapping, riding, and running. And there was quite a bit of teasing and taunting thrown in. Whenever any of the young maidens were nearby we were especially hard to control, as our war chief could tell you. I was one of the worst in wanting to be seen as the tallest, fastest, handsomest... Well, maybe some of you can remember feeling that way once."

A ripple of quiet laughter moves through us.

"About the race; as I said, we all had been preparing for months and knew it would take place around the time of the harvest dance. We also knew whoever won had a pretty good chance of catching the attention of the most beautiful maidens.

"Most of the people had been gathering throughout the week. On the day of the race you could smell the salmon, wild boar, and deer cooking in different parts of the camp. That night the harvest dance would be held, and there was a lot to do.

"Even with all of the activity, most of the people were watching us as we started the race, and I was especially glad to see that the young maidens were watching me, or so I thought. The race took us on a long stretch, winding by the river and through a high pass in the hills several miles away. We knew some of the people would be watching us at different places along the route.

"As we began my older brother, Bear, and I took the lead, but it wasn't until we got into the hills that I managed to pass him. I remember thinking that he was my toughest competition. The feeling of victory didn't last long though since several others were close on my heels. Soon the sun was falling in the west and late afternoon shadows drew long among the trees. I heard some grunting and a shout behind me at one point, but I didn't let it distract me from my purpose. It sounded a lot like some of the tricks we had pulled on each other in our summer of practice.

"On we ran, through the forest and out towards the people, all gathered at the finish point. We all burst towards the end in a tight group of legs and arms and rapid breathing. When I heard the drums and the singers, my spirits soared, and I felt the energy lift my heavy legs for a last push, just barely getting across the line before I heard the cheering. I had won the race.

"That's about the time I started strutting around like a banty rooster, practically crowing. I felt sure of my place with the young women and was already thinking about how I would look and feel at the dance. At that point I was expecting everyone to cheer for me and slap me on the back. Instead, my mother was calling out, asking for Bear. We all looked around and realized he wasn't there and that there were two others missing.

"Then things began to move fast. The alarm was sounded and those who could still run, along with some of the warriors, formed a group and went back to the hills where I had last seen my brother. I went along, exhausted. And, truth be told, I was disappointed. I expected to be the center of attention, and this was a cruel twist from my way of seeing.

"It took us a good hour to find Bear and another hour to bring him back home. He had tripped on some roots and fallen, breaking his ankle and going head first into some boulders. Two others had tumbled with him and had minor injuries. Although they were hurt, none were too badly damaged, but all three were considered the heroes of the day.

"When they returned and were bandaged up, they came to the dance. My brother was carried in on the shoulders of two of the finest warriors. It looked as if he was enjoying himself, and all the young women were drawn to him, and from my perspective paid entirely too much attention to him. Earlier I had been worried, but now I was full of anger. He had stolen my victory. He had stolen the young women. Over the evening my anger was fueled by the attention he was getting from the lingering maiden, and by the end of the night I could not contain my rage. I pushed through what was left of the people and rushed my brother. I unleashed my pent-up jealousy on him, and before I knew it several arms were pulling me off my brother.

"Now you know the worst of it, and I will tell you the rest of the story. My father's hands were the ones that finally held me, and in his eyes I saw deep coals of anger mirroring my own. In his face I also saw amazement and disappointment. That was only the beginning of my anguish, because I also saw my own stupidity and selfish ego.

"The last part of the story takes place a week later, after my brother had recovered enough to be taken along with me to a ceremony in the woods. My father had given me a task of chopping wood for a week, so I would have some time to think about my actions. Then, by the fire, he addressed us.

"'Dolphin,' he said to me, 'you have met your first enemy and it is within yourself. This time your enemy won, and from now on you must learn to tame it. Your enemy was jealousy and anger. You felt jealous and angry, and you reacted. You did not think first. You and your brother will grow to be chiefs in this life. If you are to be chiefs you must learn how to walk in balance, and you will need self discipline. Therefore you must learn now about the Circle of Law and the harmony within yourself. Self discipline is the most important element and from that will come all the others. Listen well now, for you will need this knowledge.'

"Huddled by the fire, my brother and I were so still we were like the fox on the hunt listening. As Father spoke, the hair on my arms stood on end. He had never spoken to us this way before. Every word was going in so deep it was as if we were being given something sacred. Father then began to unwrap his medicine bundle. He pulled out a shield we had never seen. Old as it was, the colors were still strong and the symbols clear. There by the fire, Father began to tell us the secrets of the Circle of Law.

"'The Circle of Law is the ancient way of balance and harmony,' he said. 'It is the way of our people and a part of how they have been able to live successfully for thousands of winters. See the symbols on this shield in front of you. They represent the energies of balance and harmony. If any of these are missing you will soon find disharmony among the people. This is true for each individual as well. Look into yourself as you hear these ancient truths. In this way you will open the self-knowledge path of understanding. This is the beginning of your training.'

"'We will start in the East of the shield,' he said pointing. There, reflected in the light of the fire, was an image of Grandfather Sun. 'This represents the spirit expressing itself. It is this freedom of spirit that must be protected, and you must create the freedom to express that spirit inside of you. This can happen in many ways. There is much to learn about this, but for now remember that without expressing spirit you will have disrespect and conflict, with no way to bring the people together.'

"I briefly reflected on my recent expression of anger and thought that it wasn't a very good example of balance. I wondered what it would look like if I could go back and relive the experience. Quickly, though, I came to attention as I realized my father was continuing.

"'Bear, what do you see here as the symbol in the Southeast of the shield?' he asked. Bear spoke that it seemed like an ancient Mayan pyramid, which looked almost transparent, like it was there and not there at the same time. We saw the oranges and yellow-reds shimmering in the light. Father spoke of our ancestors and the need to not only connect with our sense of their presence but to be able to open the door of the present. When we walk through this doorway we come into deep connection with the Universe and everything in it.

"As he was teaching us, I thought about the pyramid and wondered if it was there or not and how we might get inside of it. As I listened to his words, I hoped he had heard my silent question. He spoke about going into the stillness where we experience oneness.

"'Remember to start each day appreciating the trees and plants that give you breath,' Father said, 'and the water of the Mother that relieves your thirst. Thank the sun and fire energy that gives you heat and light and the Mother Earth who feeds you. You walk in this world among many who have come before you. Do not forget where you came from.'

"I stole a quick glance at my brother, and for an instant I saw the chief he would become. I wondered what I looked like sitting there. I hoped no sign of the banty rooster remained.

"'What do you see here, Dolphin?' I heard Father ask. As I looked at the south of the ancient shield, I saw many plants and trees, and emerging from them was a figure of a woman walking toward us carrying a pipe. I had heard of White Buffalo Woman and asked my father if this was her. His keen eyes focused on me for a moment, and I thought I saw a little surprise in his expression, but it quickly vanished as he continued. He spoke instead of the energy of the South in the Circle of Law.

"'There is much for you both to learn about this direction,' continued Father. 'Recognize this training will continue for many years so you can learn to be strong enough and wise enough to carry this shield. The plants you see on the shield represent the power of all growing plants, trees and flowers on the earth. Imagine the power that is behind this growth. You can learn to harness that kind of power through your emotions. This power of the emotions is an energy force in the human that can create or destroy. You must learn how to use such power. Think first. Ask what is needed. Then act! Otherwise your emotions will be like hot coals in your stomach, driving you to war. This the war chief must also learn. Know your enemy. Do not underestimate or overestimate the enemy!'

"'You, Dolphin, had a recent experience in which you met one of your enemies. What did you learn?'

"I was trembling as I stood to answer Father, but I knew this was one of many challenges he would give me, and I was determined not to give way to my own fear. I took a deep breath.

"'When I was chopping wood, Father, I had a lot of time to think,' I responded. 'I found out how much I wanted to be as good as Bear. Inside I was afraid I wasn't. So my true enemy was my own thought which said I'm not as good as he is.'

"I turned to my brother and said 'Bear, you are a good brother to me and I hope you will accept my apology to you.' Bear simply nodded and smiled. I knew from his expression that he had learned something, too. It wasn't until much later that Father taught us about White Buffalo Woman. But that is another story.

"Father pulled out some jerky for us to share and made some tea. I noticed how he looked at us, as if he was measuring how awake we were and how much we were taking in from his teaching. His scrutiny continued as he fed the fire and lit his pipe. I began to get just a little itchy as his fierce eyes settled on me.

"'So,' he said, 'what do you think of all this?' I had to search hard and deep for my voice since this was all new to me, and yet familiar. I told him so and he laughed.

"'Alright,' he said, 'since this is so familiar, tell me what this next symbol represents.'

"With my heart pounding, I saw the symbol clearly in the dancing light of the fire. It was round with black marks on it. The background was a reddish purple color and the marks made it look like a puzzle. 'It looks like some kind of a map, Father,' I said. 'But why is it in a circle? Where could it lead? Is it a puzzle?'

"For the second time by the fire that night, I saw something flash in Father's eyes, then quickly disappear. He again pierced me with his eyes as he began to speak. 'This is the symbol of the Southwest and it is called the maze. It is like a puzzle. It shows how we need to find our way to the center of the Self in our lifetime, but the center is not a destination; it is a journey. In our earth walk each of us must seek our true identity. We each must seek to know our true gift so we can make our giveaway. The maze is the symbol, which reminds us not to get lost as we search for ourselves and our dream. As a people we hold a deep sacredness around visions and dreams. They inform our sacred purpose and help us to see ourselves and our medicine power. When each person is able to discover their medicine they are more able to make their contribution to the whole, and this makes us strong as a people.'

"Finding the center of the Self seemed a challenging concept to me, and again I looked over at my brother. He had a faraway look on his face as he stared into the fire. Father addressed him. 'Bear, let your heart speak.'

"Bear continued looking to the fire and spoke. 'I am honored by your trust, Father. To be given this teaching is a sacred trust, and I hope I am worthy. I have many questions, and yet few are formed clearly enough to speak. May I speak about a feeling that comes to me as I look into the shield?'

"Father nodded and Bear continued. 'I dreamed last night. My dream took me deeply into the forest where I saw a bear by the entrance to a cave. I knew I was myself but I was also the bear. The cave was home to me. I experienced what it felt like to be the bear, to be the cave, and to be the trees and the land all at one time. It was a quiet feeling and yet it was more than that. It is hard to explain. I was inside something and a part of something in a way that is different from what I experience as a human. When I look at this shield and hear your words that same feeling returns. This is what my heart says, Father.'

"Hearing my brother's words made me think how much I needed to learn. Father merely nodded his head as he smoked his pipe and for once his eagle eyes focused on my brother, and he spoke again.

"'All of these symbols on this shield open the door to a deeper remembrance that is a part of our heritage. Let us speak of the one shown in the West. The symbol is our Grandmother Earth. This image in the West helps

us remember our relationship with her. We walk on this planet each day of our lives. We are form and substance like her. Our blood flows like her rivers, our systems in the body are interconnected like her plant families. She nurtures us with her breath, her rain, her sun and her body. If we listen she teaches us to care for each other and her other children. As you look into the cave, you see into yourself. Introspection and intuition are your teachers. These need to be kept forward in the people's understanding or there will be little chance for harmony. We each need to create a space for quiet, to be able to go to the cave of the Self, as you did in your dream, Bear. From introspection and intuition you will learn of healing, of teaching, and how to protect and care for the children of the tribe.'

"This is the first time an alarm went off in my mind! Caring for the children? This was not my idea of being a chief. I am sure Father saw this reaction in me, as his next words seared into my mind.

"'You think warriors aren't concerned with children? You think that is women's work! Listen well, Little Fish. You have a few things to learn before you can become a big fish!'

"My face burned hot with shame. How could he read my thoughts, I wondered. Father continued.

"'Do you think you will never have any children? Or do you think you will only care about your own, as if you are not part of a tribe? Who will teach them the skills of a warrior? And who will protect them during wartime? Ah, I see you are relieved by that thought. Do you think you will only train the young men? Don't let your mother hear about it. She can out-shoot you any time. Open your mind Little Fish,' my father said as he lit his pipe again.

"I see now how I deserved that name. Unfortunately, it stuck to me for some time. At least, I thought, he hadn't named me Rooster. I saw it was time to feed the fire, and I jumped up to gather some more wood. Father was smoking his pipe, and Bear was stretching his legs. Once more we all settled down around the heat of Chemah, the fire. Father spoke again.

"'Cycles and rhythms,' I heard him say, 'are a part of everything we are and everything we see. This next symbol, in the Northwest, reminds us of all the cycles of life. Notice how the design is interwoven. What are all the cycles you can think of?'

"Bear and I looked at each other and began 'Well, the moon rising is a cycle, the tides and the seasons, the rotation of the planets, the cycle of a plant growing, and when to pick the fruit. . .' We spoke of as many as we could and Father continued.

"'What about yourself?' he asked. 'What about your own cycle of birth, growing and death? What about your cycle of learning?' We began to see how many things in life are in cycles. He spoke to us of how we are interrelated with all the energies of life and how all the cycles interrelate.

"'This is an awareness that helps us be in harmony as we become awake to what we are learning and how these changes affect the life around us,' Father said. I again saw how much I had never thought about and what a little fish I was indeed!

"'Bear, what is the next symbol?' Father asked. Bear appeared to be looking intently at the shield.

"'I see images of many animals and what looks to be a hunter,' he replied.

"'Good,' I heard Father say. 'This is an image to remind us of the power of the animal instinct. We have the ability to access a similar knowing within ourselves, only for us it comes from the heart. Learn how to access the clarity of the heartmind. Here you will find truth and the courage to act upon it. Always act from a clear heart. If you follow this way, you will be walking the path of understanding called the Way of the Human. This is also known to be a high path of consciousness. This understanding needs to be held by the people and is a vital part of the Circle of Law, which enables the harmony of the people to continue.'

"Grandmother Moon was lighting the forest as Father continued. We had come full circle, and we were now ready to open the beginning understanding of the last symbol, in the Northeast of the Circle of Law shield. I ate the last of my jerky as Bear brightened the fire. As I looked at the symbol I saw a moon, no, several moons and a lightning bolt. There were thirteen. Ah, all the phases of the moon were shown. I looked expectantly at Father.

"'This last symbol represents the movement of the moon and the power of the lightning,' he said. I felt chills run up my back and down my arms as he continued.

"'This is power that each of us can learn to access, but it is a sacred responsibility. It is a power that must only be used to protect something precious—the life force energy. Each person is surrounded with this energy, and it is a part of all life. We see it in the plants and the animals, and in the people of our tribe. Holding this power is a dedication to see that this life energy is protected. Protect the voice of the people, my sons. Each must be able to speak their truth whether all agree or not. This diversity of perspective will bring a unity and strength to the people. All challenges and problems can be made whole and the vitality renewed when we listen to the hearts of others. This last symbol anchors the shield and completes the understanding of the Circle of Law. Each of these understandings must be awakened and held by a tribe if there is to be true harmony among the people.'

"My father's words still ring in my ears. I have continued to learn from his teachings that night in the forest. I truly was a little fish then. I had a few more challenges from the rooster part of me, but now I am an old Dolphin, leaping now and then, and I offer my story as an honoring of this gathering of remembrance. I have spoken."

The people were silent for a time, taking in the magic of the images old Dolphin evoked with his story. SeedPlanter, our elder representative from east of the mountains, rises to her feet and addresses the circle.

"This teaching story we have just heard from Leaping Dolphin is very important to us," she began. "It contains the seeds that have grown the garden of harmony of our way. Hearing Dolphin's words about the tribes needing to awaken the meaning and understanding of the Circle of Law, seems to me to be a good place for us to stop," SeedPlanter said. "Let's spend some time doing just that. I propose that we spend our time together in the next eight days in conversation to open up and deepen our understanding of these shields, one by one."

Following an old practice, the circle honors the offering of a proposal by taking the time to indicate their agreement with SeedPlanter's proposal. After some discussion, agreement is reached and a small group of elders is selected to shape the flow of the activities for the next eight days, while the rest of the camp goes about preparing for the evening.

On the morning of the fourteenth day of the gathering, we are all called to the medicine wheel created in the big meadow behind the granite shelf. The elders who had been asked to plan the next eight days of the camp's activities greet the 160 members of the different tribes. As everyone is settled in the medicine wheel, Leaping Dolphin, one of elders planning this time, addresses the group.

"To carry out the proposal made by SeedPlanter yesterday we ask you all to form into eight groups of twenty representatives," announces Leaping Dolphin. "Try to have a mixture of as many tribes as possible in each group so we will have a variety of thought to share in this deepening experience.

"We ask that each group selects one of its members to be a point for the group and that each group gather at one of the eight gateways of the medicine wheel so they are all filled," says Leaping Dolphin.

With a festive air, we move about forming eight groups. Laughter and teasing are part of a light-hearted spirit as the teams select who will be the point. Although each representative knows how important and profound this old part of their culture is, everyone knows that deep learning and appreciation are enhanced by joy and playfulness, as well as serious intention. We have an expectant sense of play and adventure about this period, as the people have agreed to explore the deepening of meaning in the Circle of Law.

The elder Sacisha, who is also part of those who have planned this time, calls the groups around her to explain how they will move together in the next eight days.

"Each of the eight teams we have formed will take responsibility to guide our activity for one of the days" explains Sacisha. "Take time now in your circle to plan how you will guide all of us in this hunt for deeper understanding. Today the society in the East gateway will begin and each day thereafter another society will lead us as we move around the teaching in the sun-wise direction."

After a time for planning the great drum sounds, and the elders announce that the ceremony will begin this day with the opening of the understanding of the Circle of Law in the East. This is where there is the teaching of the Spirit of Life and the need of the people to understand freedom and the power of creativity in the health of a tribe.

The society in the East begins and calls the people to dance and sing together a round dance called "The Friendship Way." For this beginning all the children are called to join this welcoming commencement of the camp's eight days of festive renewal of learning. As we dance each person greets everyone of the circle and then is greeted by everyone else in a revolving parade of smiling faces and with a heartfelt clasping of hands. A rich warmth of belonging and joy permeates the camp circle, and all sense of separation and difference falls away as the spirit of the people rises up.

This day's beginning ushers in the next days' and nights' rich variety of activities and events. These open to the people a deeper understanding and respect for this ground of their culture called the Circle of Law.

Daily Life: Relationship With Mother Earth

Eight days pass in the ceremony, followed by a resting day and on the twenty-second day of the gathering we are once again seated in a circle on the granite shelf. The sense of time passing has shifted and expanded in the consciousness of the people. In each of our hearts has grown the strong appreciative sense of where we are and the beauty we share. *The sage is lit and passed around the circle to bless and clear the heart, and the elder Sacisha stands.*

"I am Sacisha, and I would like to speak again." She pauses. "I see that you are all nodding agreement, so I will begin.

"I thank each of you for what we have created together in these last days. Now, while we have been sharing these stories of how we have become the people and remembered our early sense of the meaning of life, I am thinking it would be good to speak of another remembrance. It is about our way of relating with Mother Earth, day-by-day. And this is important, for it is in each day that we strengthen the beauty of our way.

"Each day of my life I remember seeing our people greet Grandfather Sun. Sometimes we have done this all together, as on special ceremony days when the seasons turn, and other times we simply gathered together at the medicine wheel. But most times, coming from my lodge in the morning, I have seen the people in small family groups or couples, together or alone, dancing the slow graceful movements of the Tslagi upon the mother's breast, like myriad birds moving softly in the morning breeze, like winged prayers breathed into the dawning day.

"Then, too, I have heard distant sounds around the village, snatches of the people singing the beautiful sounds of the Twenty Count, or other songs calling the spirit of the universe to be present in the day. All around the villages of the people there are different expressions of creating a relationship of harmony so we all can walk in beauty and awareness with the energies of Mother Earth. This is a fine way to start our days, with joy and appreciation.

"Another aspect of our relationship with Mother Earth is how we see that she provides for us. She gives us our food from Her plant and animal children that we may grow strong. Her waters She bestows on us that we may assuage our thirst and cleanse ourselves. With Her breath of air She surrounds us to give us life and quickness of mind. She gives us fire and light, shared from essence stored within Her nature, so we may keep the fire of spirit bright. These things She gives freely to us. Our way is to show our gratitude and respect for Her.

"We express our gratitude by prayer and song and dance. We dedicate ceremony to Her. By expressing thanks for each thing taken, we give back to Her and the life around us.

"We show our respect by being alert to what we are being told by Her and responding. We hold to our purpose of walking the good road and caring for what has been given to us. We choose not to waste or become neglectful. By teaching our children Her wisdom ways, by listening to Her signs and learning, and by keeping a true heart and walking with honor and integrity, we show respect and love for Her.

"This is what each of us has been taught, in many forms, as the way to relate to our Mother Earth. This way gives us joy and fullness, and when we are full and in joy, it is a gift back to Her also.

"I am Sacisha, and I have spoken."

The warmth of the sun is upon the circle and the shadows of trees reach out their welcoming shade as we reflect on the abundant images of our lives as a people.

"Ho! I am Medicine Bonnet. These are good images you have spoken of this morning, Sacisha. When you spoke of our times of joy and fullness and the gifts of our Mother Earth, I thought of the many times that feeling has come to full flower by the way we live. I saw in the vision behind my eyes the brightness those times have brought us. And this good feeling has been strengthened by our further sharing, amongst our people, the images and practices from our different tribes.

"I am now standing and holding the talking stick to speak of several other ways that we have of being in relationship with the earth. It is important that we remember that the Mother Earth is alive and is always changing in Her cycles of growth. We humans, too, are always changing in our cycles of growth, and these changes bring challenges to us, which require our diligence and alertness so we may be responsive and flexible.

"I call to mind our way when there is an imbalance or danger of conflict amongst us. We have learned that it is important when we see these signs to do two things.

"The first is our practice of giving our thoughts and feelings arising from imbalance or discord to Mother Earth. This is the way we call 'burying the weapons.' When we take the time to stand upon the earth, perhaps with a tree or plant, and speak aloud the thoughts and feelings of conflict, we ask Mother Earth to take these energies into her bosom and heal them and renew the energy. We then feel lightened of our burden and less driven by these things. She has taught us that this is one of Her gifts, which begins healing and which She provides for us in our distress.

"The second thing we do at times of imbalance is to create a sacred space to sit together with the Mother Earth's healing energy and speak together, one at a time.

She has taught us to listen carefully to one another at times like this and to learn about each other as if we were walking in each other's moccasins. This relationship with Mother Earth and Her healing energy helps us when we are lost, confused, and in times of change and challenge.

"Time and again we have seen how this relationship has brought us through difficult moments and prevented us from being split apart by differences, which block our judgment. We all know well the bitter stories of those lost peoples who have neglected to honor the healing relationship Mother Earth provides for Her human children.

"One other way we have as a people I would speak of now, before I set down this talking stick. That is our way of the council. Several times I have heard this way referred to as we recount our stories of remembrance. I mention the council now to remind us that it, too, is founded on our relationship with Mother Earth as well as all the energies of the Great Spirit that is Her source. When we gather in our councils to seek wisdom or to consider a proposal we always sit upon the Mother in a circle of respect for Her. We call upon Her healing energies and we call on the Great Spirit to guide and speak through our chiefs that we may be in harmony with Her and all Her children as we ask for the wisdom to act.

"In future times, when our way is remembered again, I know it will be good that we recall this way of harmony with Mother Earth as the ground of our wisdom. Without remembrance of this healing relationship in those future times we might well destroy our world, as Grandmother reminds us in the story of the animal council. I am Medicine Bonnet, and I have spoken."

With these words, the circle nods assent to the young man's call to attention and expresses their sounds of appreciation. Singing Waters, one of the elders, speaks to the group.

"It seems to me that we have much to consider in all the stories we have heard from one another," speaks Singing Waters. "We have many riches gathered in these days. I suggest we take time now to have a council where we will gather all these treasures of memory and begin to see a pattern in them that we can carry back to our people so they will be strengthened in the times to come."

We indicate assent to this suggestion, and Pathfinder calls the people to stand.

"Ho! I am Pathfinder, and I see by our shadows on this granite shelf that Grandfather Sun is completing His journey across the sky. It would be good to light our evening fire. There is fresh meat from brother deer's giveaway and the plants brought in by our hunters and gatherers. It has been a good day speaking together of these things. Let us prepare a good meal together and feast before we go to our dreams. We will continue our journey of remembrance with time to council together, as has been suggested. Come drummers and singers, sing us an evening song as we prepare."

The moon rises over the sleeping camp with a soft silvery light, covering it like a blanket. The star firmament is brightly visible and feels especially close during this special night of dreams.

Chapter Two

Three Journeys to the Distant Past

Preparing for the Journey

The twenty-fifth day of the gathering begins as we, the people, greet the sunrise in prayerful dance and song. Yesterday we held a rewarding council that anchored the stories deeply in the representatives' memories. Now Pathfinder steps forward to speak.

"I am Pathfinder, and I see we are all gathered here again after our night's rest. Now that we have greeted the day with the dance of Tslagi and shared our morning food I will paint an image for you as we continue our journey of remembrance.

"We have had a good and meaningful time in our camp of sharing old teaching stories and of time to absorb them afresh in our days of activities. However, to complete this time of remembrance, we must journey together into our distant past. Our ancestors have important things to remind us of, old secrets of how we have come to be who we are. Let us travel in shared remembrance, then, to three different times and places from this Hill of Remembrance. We will go across time and space and in our minds revisit some of these earlier times, where our way was held by our ancestors.

"For the next three passages of Grandfather Sun we will travel to each of these three places. The first trip will be to the *Morning Star Kiva*, so the ancestor twin elders can speak to us of the Way of the Human. Second, we will travel to the ancestor elders in the distant *Star Maiden Lodge*, to hear their explanation of the Nature of Human Relationship. And, last, we will go to an old *Council Longhouse* to hear the ancient ones and open our minds to the Patterns of Thought and Action. By traveling together in this way we will turn the soil of memory so our plant of remembrance will fully flower and produce the seeds of recall that will dream of rebirth in our future.

"Before we begin, I see one of our young maidens signaling that she has some words to speak. What do you wish to say, young one with the bright eyes?"

"I am Crescent Moonlight, and I need some help for this journey you speak of, Grandfather Pathfinder," said the young maiden. "I have heeded this call of invitation to the journey of remembrance, and I have enjoyed the stories from our elders, recounting their learning journeys. I felt I was there with Elder Standing Tree and Grandmother SeedPlanter and the others when they were learning. Now, however, I hear we are going on a journey of imagination to these three exciting places where I have never been, and I want to be there too. Can anyone tell me how to travel with you this way? I am Crescent Moonlight, and I have spoken."

"Ho, I am Listening Crow," said a tall man with long dark braids. "I will speak to your question Crescent Moonlight. I remember asking the same thing when Grandmother SeedPlanter took twelve of us young ones to the ancient well of remembrance. We were traveling in our imagination for the first time. I see you smiling, Grandmother, at the memory of my youthful impatience.

"We were all sitting in a cave high up in the west mountains, waiting out a storm that caught us while we were gathering huckleberries. It was pretty cold, and we didn't have any wood for a fire. 'Alright!' Grandmother SeedPlanter said. 'While we're waiting for this cold rain to stop, I am going to take you, in your imagination, to a warm place where we will find a bright sunny meadow.'

"At this point I asked the same question you have, Crescent Moonlight. But I'm afraid I didn't ask in the same respectful way you did. I was cold and wet and grumbling with impatience when I spoke.

"'Listen to my words, little wet bird' SeedPlanter said, fixing me with her eyes. 'We are all cold here for the moment, but we have a power that can change how we experience things. It's called imagination and it's a gift from the Mystery, which gives us great freedom. Right now I want us to use this power to go to a warm place together while we wait for the rain to stop. Do you want to go with us?'

"Ashamed of my complaining, I nodded yes.

"'So here is what you do, Little Bird,' she said. 'Close your eyes when I start drumming on my hand drum. I will speak in images of the place we are going. As you hear my words, relax and let the sounds form pictures in your mind. Let yourself feel what the images create for you—smells, touches, sounds, tastes, feelings. Focus on these things and you will be there with me and the others.'

"So I did as Grandmother SeedPlanter suggested, and she took us to this beautiful place where we felt warm and experienced being with the ancient stones in the well of remembrance. I have never forgotten that journey. When Grandmother SeedPlanter brought us back, the rain had stopped, and I wasn't feeling cold. I, Listening Crow, have spoken."

"I am Crescent Moonlight, and I thank you, Listening Crow, for helping me see how I can go on this journey with Grandfather Pathfinder. I am excited to go now to the Morning Star Kiva. I have spoken."

Journey to the Morning Star Kiva

Gentle Drum
    Drumming Sound
        Heart Rhythm
            Gentle Beating

We lift from our granite shelf now. Gently, like our Eagle kin do as they rise from the limbs of the tall pines. Feel the lightness of our bodies as we see our camp circle growing smaller beneath us as we move upward into the sky. We see now the rim of mountains surrounding this Hill of Remembrance and the thin column of smoke rising from our campfire far below. See how the snow on the mountain peaks makes patterns, like fingers reaching down into the carpet of green forest.

We glide to the west now, away from the rising sun and move swiftly toward Namahiah, Grandmother Moon, as she sets on the western horizon. The long trading river unwinds below us like a great silver snake.

Ahead we begin to see the vast open plains stretching in the distance. Those black patches of shifting shape moving over the brown slopes are our buffalo relatives seeking new grass.

In front of us, like the ragged crest of the lizard's back, are the great grizzly mountains. We fly over them and come down lower on their western side.

Now, see ahead the broad ragged cracks of shadow running across the surface of the rolling plain. Those are the canyons where the ancient ones lived. They carry much of the memory of the people of the south lands and are part of the trail of our human ancestry. We glide lower now into the canyon ahead, singing in our minds the sounds of the traveling song, letting the spirits of the place know we come in a good way with peace in our hearts.

Ahead we see the high canyon walls with many vertical crevices, like folds in a hanging blanket. At the base of the canyon wall is our first destination, a multilevel structure backed up to the wall with a curved open plaza in front.

We move to the large circular shape in the center of the plaza terrace. Inside, below the ground, is the Morning Star Kiva where the ancestor grandparents await us.

We climb down the ladder which rises out of the opening in the circle. We descend with prayers into the Kiva of memory.

"I am in this delicate lodge. . . I sit before myself. . . I hear myself. . . I honor myself. . . These are words from our ancient poetry," sound the voices of the ancient grandparents.

Their beautiful, brown, weathered faces shine with wisdom, like polished burl root. The smell of sweetgrass smoke mixes with the earthen scent of the curved layered stone walls, and we have a deep sense of being surrounded by wholeness and peace. The ancient grandparents continue.

"The poetry speaks the words of our human spirit reminding us of the ground of respect that we must carry within our hearts if we are to walk the Way of the Human in our life times," echoed the ancient voices. "Look here on the floor of the Kiva. We will draw in the sand this symbol of the Morning Star. You see it is like a circle radiating light energy in the four directions.

"In the legends of the people it is spoken many times that we come from the stars," the ancient ones continued. "What we call the Morning Star is a bright planet

that travels close to us in her circling journey through the sky. But the light that is reflected from this planet is from another star, Grandfather Sun, and reminds us of our origins. We will draw here in the sand another way the people make the glyph sign of the Morning Star. As you see, this one is like a diamond. There are many ways that the people have woven, beaded, and painted this symbols, but all of them carry the remembrance of our origins, and speak to us of the Way of the Human that we hold and follow."

The grandmother and grandfather point around them with staffs, drawing attention to the beautiful designs in blankets and paintings on the surrounding walls and columns of the Kiva.

"We humans surround ourselves with symbols that help our memory to stay awake to who we are as we walk in this sacred dream we call life," speaks the grandfather.

"There are many levels to the experience we have as we move through our Sacred Dream, both in our waking time and our sleeping time," comes the voice of the grandmother. "When we speak of the illusion of the Sacred Dream, we are referring to the many levels that can be perceived in different ways as we open to our full consciousness."

"Let us speak of one example of the different levels that we all know," speaks Grandfather. "As we stand here now in this Kiva we see the stone walls and the timbered beams of the ceiling, the columns and the ground beneath our feet. These all seem solid to us, firm and hard. Yet if we close the door to the Kiva and put out the torches and sit silently in the dark for a time, the reality and firmness of these things is not with us, and other presences come to us—some of them in forms of sight, others by sound or smell, and some by a sense of presence. All this experience exists in this place. But the experience of this place occurs on different levels, and we open to our consciousness in different ways to experience these levels."

"We speak of these things so that we may open to a remembrance of one of the teachings that the symbol of the diamond glyph brings to mind," speaks the grandmother. "This is about the way to walk as the human in this illusion we call the Sacred Dream. To walk as a human is a high art of consciousness. It is because of this fact that our teachings always speak first of images of the healthy whole person, so we have a measure toward which our people can aspire in their learning and growth."

"What the grandmother has spoken is important," the grandfather adds. "To weave a beautiful blanket or to craft a fine arrow is an art. If these artists were not given a measure of excellence as they learned their skill, if they only saw crude and misshapen blankets or arrows as they were learning, then their search for beautiful expression would be hampered by having to recreate the whole art from the beginning. They would have nothing of value from the experience of those who searched before them.

"By having an image as a measure of excellence, the young student is not denied the freedom to seek their own unique discovery and creation of expression. As each of us grows up and matures, we need such a measure—of what it is to be a healthy human—to guide us in growing toward our own unique potential.

"The glyph of the Morning Star, the diamond we have drawn here in the sand, carries the information of the measure of our way of walking as a human," speaks the grandfather. "Each of the points on the diamond carries an energy that we can express in a word. Our ancestor teachers have made it clear that each of these energies must be held and combined in balance by the one who would walk the path of the human."

The grandmother steps forward, the bells around her ankles tinkling. Pointing with her staff to the South point of the diamond she speaks.

"The word for this point is *responsibility*. The energy here is the movement of stepping forward with a conscious alertness and responding to a situation. This is different from a reaction which is driven by impulse, because the energies that drive impulse are not conscious of our intelligence and the measure we used. Another way to see into this word *responsibility* is to speak it as the ability to respond.

"Our way is to train our young to not jump into action at the first stimulus, whether a situation can be seen, heard, tasted, smelled, or felt, without the presence of a still center. This still center is a condition of heightened awareness. The presence of a still center from which our actions or words flow is the beginning place and defines the character of the adult human," emphasizes the grandmother.

"By responding in this way to our life experiences we become good parents, caring lovers, skillful hunters, enlightened teachers and powerful warriors when necessary. As we train the young in this way, the time between stimulus and conscious response can be as quick as the flash of the lightening bug or as long as a walk to a distant mesa, whatever is most appropriate to the circumstance."

Now Grandfather rises from his seat and stands opposite the grandmother, taking his place at the north point of the diamond in the sand. Motioning with his staff he speaks.

"The word *choice* holds the energy of the second quality needed by one who walks the Way of the Human. In training our young we plant the seed of an attitude of worthiness to walk in self-authority in creating their life. With this comes a freedom to choose how they want to respond and to learn from the consequences of their choices. We also train the young so they know that in any given circumstance there are many possibilities to choose from and each must learn how to see the opportunities in each situation. So *choice* represents an energy that is open and seeking, combined with decisive power and follow through.

"Here is a story to illustrate the training process in *choice*," Grandfather said. "Imagine a young hunter is being tested for readiness to be adopted into the society of hunters. He is told that in three days there will be a feast for the clan to celebrate his entry into the hunting society, and that he is to provide the food for the people for that day. It is made clear that no one of the clan will eat that day unless he brings food back for the feast. The young man is given four arrows for his bow and told to go out and return on the third day.

"So this young man goes far to find a deer large enough to feed the clan. Using the tracking skills he has learned, he looks in a search pattern for spoor and tracks in the early morning. By evening he finds no recent signs of game. He has climbed canyon walls and many trees, looking for deer. In the evening of the first day he sits and sends his prayers for the deer to give away. The first day passes, and the second day begins to wane when he comes to a small water hole surrounded by bushes. As he creeps up he sees a slight movement through the bushes. Peering through, he sees a buck with horns lowering his head and drinking from the pool. With a prayer to the deer in thanks, he notches and releases his arrow. At the same moment he is startled by a shout. Running into the clearing by the pool he finds the buck lying on its side, but a strange arrow shaft is protruding. Just then a tall warrior from a distant clan steps through the bushes with a shout of triumph. He points to the young hunter and says, 'This deer has given

away to me for my people. Why do you stand here with a look of possession on your face?'

"The young hunter tells the warrior that he had released a true arrow with prayers and that it was his arrow that brought down the buck. He lifts the buck and points to his arrow, broken but protruding from the heart place. 'This buck has given away to me for my people, and I so claim it!' shouts the young hunter.

"'That is not the way it will be young one,' the warrior replies, drawing his knife.

"In this moment the young hunter saw he must choose. He stopped the rising tide of fear and anger, and in the still moment he reached for his bag of prayer tobacco rather than his knife.

"'Let us offer prayers of thanksgiving together for the spirit of our brother deer and seek the meaning for both of us in his giveaway,' says the young hunter quietly. 'If we spill each other's blood here over our brother deer it will neither honor the gift nor bring a blessing to our people.'

"For a long moment the tall warrior gazes with intensity into the young hunter's eyes. Then a broad smile spreads across his face as he speaks.

"'You have chosen well, young man. I see you are seeking more than this brother deer for your people this day. We'll do as you suggest and seek the meaning of our two arrows taking this giveaway.'

"So the warrior and the young man offered prayers of thanksgiving and sat to council together. As a result the warrior brought several of his clan to join the young man in skinning the deer, and they all carried it back to the young man's clan. The warrior and his clan members joined in the feast honoring the young man's adoption into his hunting clan. After the celebration both clans' hunting societies joined in a hunt for their clans, and a new alliance between the two tribes was formed.

"The choice the young man made in the moment of contest over the deer became a story told many times around the campfires of the people. The tale of the young man's action and the consequences became a teaching subject for the young men and women of the clan.

"I know this story well," the grandfather continued, "for the young hunter was my father's father. The story speaks to us of the significance of a moment's choice and the courage of the heart to take the right action. It also speaks to us about taking action from a center of stillness rather than being driven by impulse."

Now the grandmother moves to the east side of the diamond. She draws a line in the sand with the tip of her staff, from the south to the north of the diamond.

"What we have spoken of," she says, "are two of the aspects needed for the individual to walk as the human, *response-ability* and *choice*. Freedom of the spirit to manifest itself is in both of these aspects, for the spirit wishes to create and must not be limited by the dictates of impulse or the sense of being excluded from all possibility. Now we will speak of two other aspects held in this design of consciousness.

"One is here in the east of the diamond, where I now stand. Here is the aspect we call *discernment*. Opposite in the west of the diamond, where the grandfather has moved, is called *will*. I will speak first of the aspect of *discernment* and then grandfather will speak of *will*. Both of these give power for the human's arrow of intention to move to action.

"What do we mean by *discernment*?" asks the grandmother, looking around the circle of people. "In our way we know that we humans are part of a mystery, a great ocean of energy, and we are like drops of water in this great ocean. We are not separate from this ocean of energy. We are made of it and are related to it in every moment. We are formed of this mystery, touched by it, shaped by it, breathed into by it, and are part of its constant song. It is like the sounds that blend in the people's song of appreciation when they sing together. So it has always been from the beginning. We are sensitive to disharmony, not only in song, but in all things of this mystery of life. It is of this sensitiveness to harmony and disharmony that we speak when we speak of *discernment*.

"To develop our sensitivity to the presence of harmony or disharmony is part of the necessary consciousness of those who would walk as humans. When we become insensitive to disharmony, whether it be emotional, physical, mental or spiritual, we do not allow ourselves to face our pain. Instead we carry it as a burden, and we experience resentment or irritation. And if we fail to ask questions about what is needed to change disharmony to harmony, we become caught in a trap of powerless inertia. If we are not sensitive to the presence of harmony when disharmony is present, we fail to understand the nature of this energy, and we lose the ability to create it. So we must ask ourselves, what consequences can we discern? Will our action support harmony or disharmony?"

"The fourth aspect of this measure of human consciousness is the energy called *will*," says the grandfather. "It is placed in the west of the diamond. One who wants to walk as a human needs to understand that the humans are only one of myriad forms of life expressed by the Great Spirit, Wakan Susquann. All that we see and know flows from this Great Mystery and all of these things carry the seed of energy from the Great Spirit and are sacred. This is the one great relationship from which all others derive. This is the will of life and this *will* is in all things.

"To walk the Way of the Human that is reflected in this diamond of consciousness, the will of the individual person must seek the wisdom to walk a path of harmony with all of life. To walk the Way of the Human is to walk with humility and seek the wisdom to align our will in harmony with the Great Spirit," said the grandfather in a deep and quiet voice.

"We have reminded you of the Morning Star, as a seed we hold, which was planted in us in the beginning," speaks the grandmother. "Four points on a diamond of remembrance.

**Qualities of the Human:
Ring of Power**

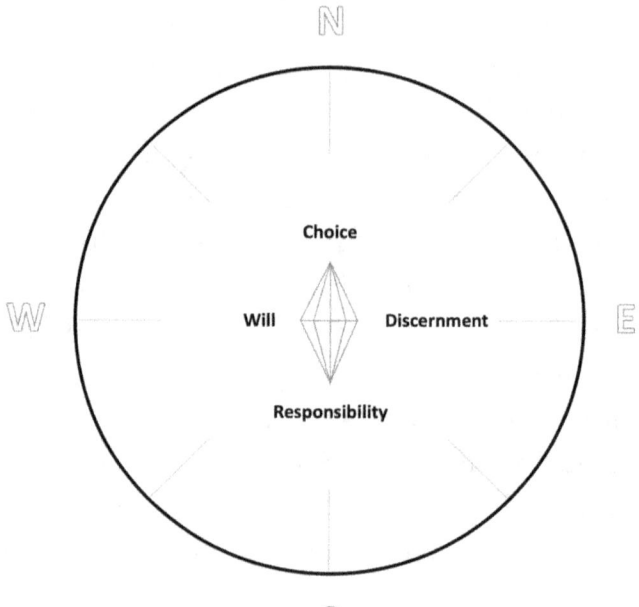

This remembrance our people have called the 'Ring of Power.' Holding this understanding consciously has enabled the people to walk the path of Beauty."

The old grandmother and grandfather sing the beauty song, rattling and drumming as we ascend the ladder through the opening in the roof of the Kiva. With their song in our ears we begin our journey back to the Hill of Remembrance.

We are challenged to reconnect with our present surroundings as we had been so deeply present in the Morning Star Kiva. As we open our eyes and find ourselves here in the circle on the hill, we see Grandfather Sun about to travel below the horizon.

The natural sounds of the camp make a soft rumble as the people settle in for the restful evening ahead. Some gather more wood for the many small fires, and others start the cooking, while some of the elders are content to sit and muse.

Journey to the Star Maiden Lodge

The evening passed gently, and the people awaken rested and refreshed. We listen to Pathfinder as we begin our next journey.

"This dawn we will continue our journeys of remembrance by traveling to the Star Maiden Lodge, far into the deep forests of the northeast on the edge of the great river leading to the eastern waters. Before we lift our consciousness again from our granite shelf, here on the Hill of Remembrance, let me remind you to awaken your perception as the images form themselves. See in your mind the detail; smell and taste the pungency of life; experience the sounds and feelings evoked from the images painted in your mind. This way our remembrance will be anchored more securely in the texture of our collective memory.

Lifting now on wings of thought, we see our camp recede and grow smaller below us. We turn in flight to the left of the rising sun and soar over the snow-covered dreamer peaks and across the forested valleys, which spread in every direction. On the horizon is the old eastern range of mountains, drawing rapidly closer. As we glide over the forested mountain crests and descend the sunlit slopes, we see many villages with morning fires where the people are preparing meals for the beginning of their day.

Ahead is the broad river flowing toward the big water, which shines on the horizon. Several large canoes move across the river toward the gray cliff walls that line this part of the river like palisades. Now we dip down in our flight, among the large branched trees, and come to the center of a clearing, to a large conical-shaped wigwam covered with the bark of the white birch.

"This is the Star Maiden Lodge, and the grandparents await," says Pathfinder.

We stoop to enter the low door and speak our prayer, 'all my relations,' reminding ourselves of our connection to the sacred web of life. We pass inside, and the fruity smell of birch mixes with herbs and fresh pine, drawing us to remembrance from the past.

> "When we are born,
> we are born into the dream,
> now we seek ourselves in the dream."

These are the first words of the ancestor twins, the grandparents, standing by the fire in the Star Maiden Lodge. Hearing this ancient poetry calls us to the time of the distant past, and we listen as the grandmother speaks.

"You are spirit beings. Before you were born you made a choice to come to this earth, to be in form, and to remember yourself in this life walk. You are each a part of the Sacred Hoop. The Hoop is the great circle connection which holds all humans of every color, heritage and culture. All those who have lived, are living, or will live are a part of the Sacred Hoop. We pray for the mending of the Sacred Hoop, the healing of the Human Family. Know we are holding you as you learn and grow in your life.

"Our people knew that all things in our life are meant to teach us. Each event, each situation, and all the things that happen in our lives are a part of a mirror that is showing us what we need to learn. We only need to pay attention. This is hard for us at times since it is true that as humans we sometimes would rather not know. Then we ignore the lessons and the opportunities to learn until something serious happens. This is usually when we start to pay attention and begin to develop our awareness.

"In this life walk, we are like the traveler walking the mountain path. See the path as it winds around the great mountain. Your path is your own and you walk it alone, yet there are times you will have companionship on your journey. Be awake, however, as not all companions will help you find your way; some will try to encourage you to go with them on their path. This is how you can get lost. You must find your own path. It is up to you. Each time you circle the mountain you open a new cycle. Be aware of the cycles of your life. Stop now and then, and remember where you have been and what you have learned. This will help you to see where you are going.

"Your actions are important. Each one has meaning. Your thoughts are important. Each one affects the whole. Your words are important. Each time you speak, your thoughts take form and become a part of the whole. We are not isolated beings. We are not separate from all that we see and know. We are part of a whole. We are a part of the web of life and related with all other humans, plants, and animals. We are related in that we are all children of the earth and the sun. We are each like drops in the great ocean. Let this speak to our identity.

"I am a drop of water.
I am the great mother ocean.
I am both.
I am a part of all.
I am the breeze, the wind, the hurricane,
    and I am the single breath of life.
I am heat and light,
    and I am the fire.
I am a single grain of sand,
    and I am the whole earth.
I am myself,
    and I am all.
I am in this life,
    and life is in me.
We are one."

Grandfather spoke next. "By this fire in this lodge I have had a vision of our future. Listen and I will tell you what I have seen. Listen so we can remember in that future.

"You are planting a field. You are planting in the west of the field. You have removed all of the debris. You have turned over the soil and planted your seeds with prayer and intention. You have sung to the seeds of their journey to come and reminded each of them of their destiny. You notice for the first time that there is someone who is in the east of the same field. They are not planting. They have built a machine that goes deep into the ground and they seem to be searching for something under the surface. The machine is digging and has a rocking motion. It never seems to stop. Day and night it rocks. There are many other mechanical things on wheels moving over the field. Debris is everywhere.

"You look to the south. In the distance you see great mounds of rock and something black and shiny. You see humans around these mounds, and they seem to be covered with this black substance. There is great activity with many machines and many people. There is no planting. Waste is all around.

"You look to the north of the field. There are many buildings and pathways. The pathways are wide and flat. They look black and shiny. Many machines travel these pathways. The sky color is brown, and it is hard to breathe. There are many people. There are no animals. There is no planting. This is what I have seen in the fire.

"The earth planet is like this field," Grandfather continued. "In what I have seen in our future, many all over this earth are planting their thoughts and their ideas in the field. We all share the same field. We all live on the same Mother Earth. We affect each other. What effect will the machines have on the planting? What effect will the mounds have on the waters? What effect will the dwellings and huge cities have on the animals that live in that place? These are things we will face in the years to come. What, then, will we need to remember?

"Our connections and the way we affect each other are sometimes hard to see, like the spider web. Our thoughts are like the silver thread of the web. We can create beauty or we can destroy. What is our destiny? This is a question each of us must answer ourselves."

We are quiet, listening and seeing the images painted in our minds. Soon the old ones begin again.

"I will tell you a story of the Killing Winter," spoke the grandmother. "In my younger days I was a traveler on the mountain path of my earth walk. I had walked for over 30 summers, and I had many children. It was good. There had been many times of challenge on the journey but like the willow tree I had learned to become stronger with each one, until the Killing Winter. That is when I met the great kachina of tragedy.

"Our tribe had planned to winter in the mountains near Twin Peaks. It had been a long journey, and we were all deeply worn, nearing exhaustion. We had met several of the white traders on our way, and later many of our people were feeling a strange illness creeping deeper and deeper into their bones. The winter became very hard as the wind carried the cold rain and snow like an icy arrow into our hearts. Without words we began to set up our shelters and to search for the nearest kindling to start our fires. We needed most of all to be warm and to rest. We had no food left after our long journey, only a few herbs, and after setting up our shelters we made our fires. As I looked around, the ones who had run out of strength simply fell asleep in their wet clothes. Days and nights all ran together as each of us slowly fell to the sickness, consumed by fever. Those who could tried to help the young ones, who were the most vulnerable.

"In the first week we lost over 50 of our young people, and we didn't even have the strength among us to give them a burial ceremony. I don't know how I stayed alive during that terrible time. I only know when the shocking reality hit me, I wished I hadn't. We had begun as a strong people of over 400. After that winter, we were 12. My entire family had gone on to the Great Round. After the winter blanket had lifted and the new spring began to emerge, we cared for those whose spirits had traveled on.

"I felt as if my spirit had left. I felt abandoned and alone. I had seen my will fall to the ground, flowing as a river of tears into the darkness of my grief. Slowly I became more and more distant, and I began to lose my sanity. I would eat nothing. I had chosen to follow my family.

"But as you can see, that was not to be. The only surviving grandmother came to me each day with her earth teas and her chanting, calling my spirit back. For many days and nights I simply closed my ears, and then somehow her heart song pierced my wall of sorrow and I began to listen. She sang this song to me.

"She said I was a traveler on this earth walk. That I would meet many kachinas on this walk, and each one would teach me. Some would be hard and some would bring beauty. She taught me that wherever I was on my journey there would be those who had gone ahead of me and those who would follow. She said she was one of the ones who had gone out ahead of me, who had traveled this way and was there to help me continue to climb. And, if I chose to live, she said I would be accepting the responsibility to help others who came after me. She taught me there were no accidents; that in some way, at some level, each of us had called the mirrors of life to us, so that we could reveal the truth to ourselves.

"It was then that I knew for certain that my life was not over. I had more to do. I have lived over 95 summers in my time and met many who needed the gift I had received. I pass it on to you now for you to carry to those you meet on your earth walk. This is our way," the grandmother said. "We are here to make this giveaway. It is a part of our destiny to learn and to remember and to share that with others."

Again we are still as the images of the Killing Winter dance in the flames of the fire. And once more the grandmother speaks.

"I will tell you the Star Maiden story so you will understand. Long ago in the distant past, there was a daughter born of a Star Chieftain. She was very beautiful and shone brightly. The day came when she noticed the beauty of the earth planet. She fell in love with this beauty and yearned to travel there. When she asked her father, the Star Chief, he said it was not time yet for her to make this journey.

"Time passed. Once again she gazed on the beauty of the earth planet and felt her yearning. This time when she approached her father, she said it was now time for her to make the journey to the earth. As he loved his most beautiful star daughter he consented but made her agree to return when he called her. Gratefully she accepted the condition and began her preparations.

"She lived on the earth for many summers and there found her love, a handsome warrior, who in time became her mate. Together they had a beautiful daughter. They lived many happy years together. After this child had grown into a beautiful young maiden, her mother heard her father, the Star Chieftain, calling for her to return home. She knew then the time had come to share the Star Maiden Wheel with her daughter. It was to be her gift to the people of the beautiful planet earth. She taught her daughter that she must teach the Star Maiden Wheel to the people, so they can live in harmony with their star relatives.

"This is our way of relationship," the grandmother spoke firmly. "Listen to this ancient wisdom.

"The first point of the Star teaching is of the need to find and remember our Sacred Dream. The Star Maiden taught the people that the Sacred Dream will continue to unfold as we travel on our mountain path of life. She taught there will be many times when we need to renew the dream symbols as the cycles of our lives will take us to new places in ourselves.

"The second point she taught was that we are here to learn and grow and actively seek our learning as we journey and that life is always teaching us. This is a powerful way to walk as we journey in our lifetime. What are we here to learn? What we discover as we begin to awaken to the many ways of responding to this question will guide our inner ability to shape our giveaway.

"The Star Maiden taught that the way we hold ourselves and our way of being is important. In this next point, she described the dance of beauty as the rainbow movement of our energies manifesting in balance. The playfulness of the dance of energy can bring the magic alive in us like the wind playfully moving the leaves of the tree. We each have a magic within us that can emerge when we begin to see how to balance our own energy in all the ways we manifest ourselves.

"How we see ourselves and how we are able to keep our spirit open to our own developing nature was, and always will be, a point on the star that we each need to learn. How can we continue through all kinds of conditions to fill our thoughts with appreciation, no matter what we see and hear and experience? I have studied this for 95 summers," said the grandmother, "and have begun to understand what this means. It is the basis of self respect.

"The next point on the star teaches us about the yearning of our spirit to express itself. Our spirit is like a great geyser, emerging from deep in the earth. If that force is suppressed it is like shutting off the source of our power to create, to imagine, and to vision.

"Through memory and the story of the ancestors' journeys we can understand the spirit of adventure and how it affects our ability to open to life. This next point on the star reminds us to be seekers, to embrace the energies of curiosity and discovery, which will awaken the awe and wonder of the little child in us. In this way trust is born in our hearts, and then—and only then—can we experience the true nature of life.

"We walk in this dream of life. We are the dreamers, and we are the dream. We are the weavers, and we are the woven ones. As we journey in life, the Star Maiden taught that we need to learn to care for ourselves, for each other, and for the sacred Mother Earth. This point is the seed of the Star Maiden teaching of relationship. We must always seek to care for the self first, then to care for others. For what good are we if our balance and well being is lost while we give and give? Eventually we become like the dry well.

"Listen. Listen to your own heart. This is the final point on the star," sang the grandmother. "Learn to hunt the silence, for there you will find the quiet stream of stillness. In the stillness you will discover the truth and reveal the way forward. This clarity of knowing belongs to each of us. Early in our life walk, it is easy for us; this knowing comes naturally to us, like our four-legged teachers. As we grow older, however, we begin to forget our own ability, and we must become the hunter to reclaim what is ours."

Grandfather speaks next of his joy in seeing us, and he asks us to carry the remembrance of each of them. They sing the journey song to us as we say our good-byes and offer our gifts of tobacco for their pipes.

Our journey to the Star Maiden Lodge comes to an end after the grandparents speak their final words and begin their song. The mem-

ory remains as we open our eyes and take in the sunset, illuminating each of our faces as we sit, consciously again, on the granite shelf. This day of remembering has given each of us a powerful gift to carry forward into the future.

Journey to the Council Longhouse

"We are here now, once again, in our circle on the Hill of Remembrance, having visited two of our destinations of recall," said Pathfinder. "The first was to the Morning Star Kiva to hear our ancestor elders speak to us about the Way of the Human, and the second was to the Star Maiden Lodge to hear the ancient ancestor grandparents speak to us of the Nature of Relationship. From each of these journeys we have deepened our remembrance of our way of walking on the Mother Earth. This strengthening of our collective memory is good so that we can bring this back when the people return in the future.

"This day we will journey to the third of our destinations. On the wings of imagination we will fly to a place in the east where one of the many Council Longhouses of the people has heard the voices of deliberation for many bundles of years. As we go to this gathering place it is good to be aware that the people have gathered to seek wisdom in many places and ways during our history, like the deer over time going to the countless lakes to drink the waters of life."

Ho, we rise up into the sky. Our camp is a distant circle below as we fly toward the rising sun. Dense forest, flashing streams and waterfalls pass beneath us. We pass over another part of the old eastern mountains covered with wispy tails of fog that looks like prayerful smoke.

Ahead of us spreads a vast lake shaped like a huge canoe, four walking days in length. Beyond the lake we see a large land bordered by the big waters. We fly low now, over the bay waters, coming to the land where there is an inlet bordered by tall reeds. Thousands of geese relatives fly up at our approach and we see the shape of the longhouse through the trees. We see ahead the council longhouse set in the middle of the village. Poles holding the thatched siding of the lodge extend into the sky providing a large space for many families to share a sleeping place and to share the council fire.

Entering the longhouse, we see a natural living space, which holds many individual family sleeping areas separated by skins, and a large central area where we see the elders sitting by the fire. Smoke holes open in the roof above, allowing the smoke to escape. We each find our places around the fire and take in the beautiful smells of sage, cedar and pine. We hear the words of the grandfather.

"When you see me here,
you see nothing.
When you see yourselves here,
you see everything.
These are words that are a part of our ancient poetry. I will tell you what they mean to me.

"I was a young chief, and I had a lot to learn. I was impressed that I had become a chief after only 30 summers and had many important words to say when we sat in council. My father, Moon Walker, was a quiet man and a good listener. When you sat with him you knew that he was really there with you, and he seemed to have all the time in the world to look into whatever it was you wanted to talk about. He told me that listening was a good way to learn the true nature of those around you. He said if I really respected the person I was listening to, I would ask questions and reflect deeply on the message that was being given. The reflections needed to be taken seriously, since this was the source of wisdom, and sometimes this took time. He said I needed to learn patience.

"Then my father began to speak of the old chiefs and how they were holders of the well-being of all the people. 'Imagine,' he said, 'that I was given a very beautiful bowl. The bowl's history was important, as well as the hands that made it and the way the clay was gathered from the Mother Earth. The clay had taken hundreds of years, in the place by the riverbed, to become fine and strong. The one who gathered the clay sang sacred songs in ceremony before going to the place of the clay. When she went to gather the clay she offered prayers of gratitude for the clay makers and asked for permission to use the clay for a sacred purpose.'

"'After the clay was gathered, it was carried to the bowl maker. The bowl maker prayed that he would be worthy of his responsibility and would honor the gift of the Mother Earth to make a beautiful bowl, especially this bowl, since it would be a sacred listening bowl for use in council. He prayed and dreamed for four days and nights, fasting and drinking only water as he asked for the vision and the power to create the bowl.'

"'After his ceremony he began to sing his vision song calling to the spirit guardians of council to guide him as he crafted the bowl. He then worked for four days to create the most sacred bowl of his life. All the time it dried, and as he prepared the fire for the kiln, he held it in his thoughts. Being in the kiln was the most challenging time. It was when the bowl would come through the fire to be purified and strengthened for its sacred purpose.'

"'Later, taking it from the kiln, he brought the colors of the dawn to the bowl. And before he fired it once more, he prayed and called upon all his spirit helpers to guide his hand. This bowl was the greatest work he had ever created. After 65 summers of working with clay he was satisfied and humbled by the experience. Now it was ready to be blessed by Namahiah, the Moon Grandmother, and by Grandfather Sun on the dawn of the winter solstice. He carried it to the highest hill and awaited the sunrise.'

"'This is the story of the bowl,' my father said to me. 'The bowl has been carried by our family for all the people for 300 summers. Now you must accept this sacred responsibility to become the keeper of the bowl.'

"When my father, Moon Walker, finished his story he looked at me expectantly, and I asked tentatively, 'Is there really a bowl like that, Father?'

"He answered my question with another question. 'What do you think the story of the bowl means?'

"I had to reflect deeply for some time before I spoke. 'It makes me think of the council itself,' I said. 'I can imagine that the council is really the bowl. That it has been crafted and worked and rubbed over hundreds of years like in the story of the bowl. It is a sacred responsibility that we carry to search for the wisdom deep within us and to do that we must listen deeply, not only to ourselves but to each heart and spirit that is speaking, even if we don't like what is being said.'

"This was a beginning point of deeper understanding in my time as a chief and leader and important to my becoming an elder for our clan. I had many challenging times remembering the lesson my father had given me, and the image of the bowl helped me many times. I learned that any one of us could break that bowl by not listening or not honoring the truth of what was being spoken. It was not a physical bowl but a sacred energy container that we created with our prayer and with our intention. In that prayerful space we call the spirits to help us see what was needed for the benefit of all. This was the true responsibility of the chiefs in council—to hold everyone in the whole society in the bowl. It was to hold the well being of all in our hands. A high level of integrity is needed to do this. These words I speak in respect of my father, Moon Walker, and of all those who have walked before me," completed the old grandfather.

We hear a soft chanting as the grandfather finished, and the sound seems to intensify. With her hand on her heart the grandmother looks into our eyes and, it seems, into our hearts. She is shorter than the grandfather by at least three hands and is wrapped in layers of garments, with the outer covering a beautifully embroidered shawl. Her hair is pure white and tied so it falls down her back. Her hair frames a face of ancient lines and deep set eyes, which hold us as we listen to her chanting.

She ends her chant, and a deep silence falls on the longhouse. The grandmother seats herself on a beautiful blanket and invites us to sit around her.

"I am going to tell you a story that happened when I was a young girl. I was sitting in this longhouse with my people then, just as you are now. It was a time of my learning, and I share it with you. There was a powerful medicine woman who had traveled from the west many days to be with us. Many of her tribe had gathered to hear her speak."

The grandmother's words were flying across the fire and into us, like well-placed arrows. With her hand on her heart, she continues.

"'It is here that truth resides,' said the medicine woman. 'So now we will see. I call each of you to speak the truth to me. Who are you?'

"Her beautiful old face challenged us to speak. The people were looking at each other and back to the old medicine woman grandmother. And again we heard her call for truth, and she repeated her challenge question!

"Someone said, 'I am a warrior,' and someone else said, 'I am a healer.' But before any of the others could speak, the old medicine woman's voice rang out.

"'No! That is what you do. I didn't ask what you do, I asked who you are! Now I repeat: Who Are You?'

"We were silent as the people looked at the old medicine woman. She seemed as if she had grown; her power was immense. At that moment a young girl stood up. She looked about ten years old, and she stood across the fire from the old medicine woman.

"'I am a girl,' she said. We all held our breath as the medicine woman also stood.

"'Yes, and what else, little one?'

"This girl looked back at the medicine woman with an open face. 'I am a human being,' she said.

"'Yes,' spoke the medicine woman. 'This is true. And there is more to who you are. Can you tell me?'

"The girl looked into the old woman's face and saw a smile there. This gave her courage, and she took a breath and spoke once more. 'Well, Grandmother, could it be that I am Life?'

"Once again, we listened in the stillness of the silence, waiting for the medicine woman's reply.

"'Ho, Granddaughter, you are wise,' she said. 'You have given wings to the truth in your heart and let it fly out to meet me here at the fire. Come sit beside me as I tell you the story of the Circle of Foxes.'

"We all leaned forward to listen as the old one nestled the young one, like a baby bird under her wing. These are her words.

"'Once there was a people who were lost and living in disharmony. They had forgotten who they were. They knew they were in danger, so they decided to call the Dog Soldiers. They asked for help. The Dog Soldiers, who were pledged to protect the people, told them to pack their things and took them on a journey into the mountains. There all the people were told to create their camp and gather by the fire. When this was accomplished they were told to tell their story to one another. This took a full night and a day, as there were many people. When complete they told the soldiers they had done what was asked.'

"'Again they were told to tell their story. So the people began again. They noticed, however, that the stories were not exactly the same this time. Upon completion, they told the soldiers they had done what was asked, and again the soldiers said 'Tell your stories again!' This time the people were annoyed, feeling of course that they had done this already. A few of them complained but they were met with a fierceness from the Dog Soldiers, and they saw they were surrounded by them.'

"'So once again, they told their stories around the fire. This time the stories were very different, and the people became suspicious of each other. They challenged each other, yelling, shouting, and calling each other liars. The Dog Soldiers had to come to calm the people, and with the soldiers present at the fire, the people were told to continue. Now the people were angry. They felt they had done what was asked and they were frustrated. This was not helping them to create harmony and become a people together, they grumbled. They wanted to go home. But the Dog Soldiers held fast and ordered the people to tell their stories yet again.'

"'They said, 'You will tell your stories for 44 days.' Some of the people still wanted to fight each other, and some wanted to fight the Dog Soldiers, but they knew they could not win. So, very reluctantly, they began to tell their stories again, but this time something different happened.'

"'The people began to listen in a new way. They began to hear each other's hearts speaking the truth, and they began to realize that there are many layers and levels of the truth. They saw that with each telling, there is a revealing of deeper and deeper levels of truth. Now the people began to recognize each other. They began to understand each other, and they began to remember each other. They learned once more how important it was to hear each story, each one's voice. They began to understand that they each carry a part of the story and a portion of the truth. And they remembered that without all the parts of the story, the whole truth cannot be known.'

"'After 44 days together they were a people again and they knew who they were. The Dog Soldiers told them it was time to return to their home.'

"We felt we had each taken a journey to that mountain camp with the Dog Soldiers. We were mostly silent as the fire was tended and the people readjusted themselves. Soon the old medicine woman grandmother spoke again. This time she spoke to all of us.

"'You have heard the story called the Circle of Foxes. So now I will ask you, what have you learned about truth?'

"Some of us felt the fire seem to grow a little hotter at that moment. And then the voices of the people began to speak.

"'Ho, Grandmother. Thank you for your teaching story. I learned that there are many levels of truth, and that in order to be together in unity we need to remember our true identity and share what is hidden deep inside of us.'

"'Grandmother, your words touch my heart and help me remember what I need to do to come back in harmony with those I love. When we share the deeper elements of our truth we begin to come closer in understanding.'

"The voices continued while the old medicine woman sat and listened. Finally, the people were quiet again, and the little girl sitting with the medicine woman asked to speak.

"'Grandmother, you have told a good story and the people have listened, as I have. You have taught us about truth and how to be a people. But I think you have taught us something more. It is about the heart. I know mine is feeling it will burst right out from my chest, and I don't know why. Can you tell me, Grandmother?'

"And so once more the old medicine woman spoke to us. 'When you speak from the heart,' she said, 'you speak the truth. And when you awaken the energy of the heart-mind there is an opening of the heart center. This is what you feel now. It is our way to walk the path of the human. If we are on this path, we are conscious of our thoughts, words, and actions. And each of these reflect the truth of our being.'

"At that point, the old medicine woman began to use her rattle and sing the song of beauty. We all knew the song and there were many who were humming with her.

I walk with beauty all around me,
    as I walk the beauty way.
I walk with beauty all around me,
    as I walk the beauty way.
I walk with beauty before me,
I walk with beauty behind me,
I walk with beauty above me,
I walk with beauty below me,
I walk with beauty all around me,
    as I walk the beauty way.
I walk with beauty all around me,
    as I walk the beauty way.
May all my thoughts be beautiful,
May all my words be beautiful,
May all my actions be beautiful,
As I live my life the beauty way.

"This is the teaching story I received as a young woman in this very longhouse," said the old grandmother. "I share it with you who have come to gather remembrance of our ways."

We see the old keepers of this longhouse rise and stand before us. We have been given much to carry back and we speak our words of gratitude and offer small gifts to the grandmother and grandfather. They sing us a traveling song as we leave the longhouse and begin our journey back to the Hill of Remembrance.

Flying over the bay and the mountains, the waterfall and the reeds lining the river, we make our way back to the granite shelf. Now it is sunset and we each are aware of the gifting we received in this time.

"It is hard to believe we came to the Hill of Remembrance only days ago," says Pathfinder. "Wehomah the Wind called the elders to speak, preparing us as a people to carry our memories into the future.

It seems that through the elders' stories the past has come alive. Somehow we have lived and died in those stories. We have found a way to our origins and have rediscovered what we knew and held as a people.

"When we began the stories we were simply listeners, and through the telling we became alive in them and knew our own journey. Each of the teachings from the elders became our learning. We remembered.

"When we journey back to our people we will carry these memories as a new understanding. They belong to us now, and we will sit around our fires and tell them again. They will not fall to the ground.

"I have spoken," said Pathfinder.

Slowly the people find their way to their dreams, knowing sunrise will signal the beginning of many days of travel back to their many tribes. In this last night the chiefs of the people find their way to the council fire. While the people sleep they sit long into the night, reflecting deeply and connecting with the silent Mystery. They pass the sacred pipe, and with the rising of the moon Standing Tree speaks.

"It is good that we have come here. We have remembered. The awakening of our collective memory will be carried now like a live ember for the fire—protected, cherished, honored."

"It is so," spoke SeedPlanter, the grandmother from the East, "and like each of you sitting in this time of silence by the fire, I see what we have created here is only the first half of a longer journey. I have felt your thoughts and know we are aligned. More is needed. We must be able to see the needs of the people in the future." Silence followed as her words were held.

"This is clear to me as well," spoke Leaping Dolphin. "While remembering our journey and what we have learned is essential for those who will travel on through the long years ahead, we must as well have some clear vision of the needs of the future."

As each looks into the fire, the Old Man and the Old Woman Dreamer Chiefs make ready to speak. The Old Man begins to chant and the Old Woman brings out her rattle. The sounds they make seem to come from the earth and are heard deeply within each heart. The Old Man speaks.

"We have foreseen this need and have anticipated this time. We have made this journey here to bring a summons from the far north. The time has come for the Chiefs of The Many Nations to enter the sacred willow lodge."

The Dreamer Chiefs speak of the way of the dreamers and make clear they will prepare for those who choose to answer this summons and come for the ancient dreaming ceremony. They ask for twenty chiefs, a sacred number, and say that a balance of men and women are needed for the ceremony.

Each of the chiefs there by the council fire makes their own decision on that long night. Traveling into the North, to the land of the dreamers, is not only an honor, it is a responsibility and one that is not chosen lightly. The dreaming ceremony will open the doors into the Mystery and allow them to travel to the future in the dreamtime, bringing back the needed information of what the people will face and how they can prepare. Slowly, one by one, the chief's voices are heard.

"I will go."

"I will undertake this journey."

"I will travel to the far north."

Twenty voices are heard before the moon sets and the chill of the pre dawn calls them to the new day.

part Two
The Journey of the Chiefs

Chapter Three
The Dreaming Ceremony

The Departure

The tipi glowed like a beautiful lantern in the darkness of the night. Silent shadow figures were cast on the walls of the tipi from the light of the fire within. One by one the shadows rose and moved to the door of the lodge to emerge like ghostly shapes in the light of the half moon. Graceful, they drifted in single file to disappear into the dark forest wall. Two figures were watching from the edge of the forest.

"There are 20 of them, Uncle," whispered the young man. "Who are they?"

"They are the Chiefs of the Nations who have gathered here. They have been summoned to go on a journey," answered the man as he watched the last figure glide into the forest.

"Uncle, I get the feeling something very important is happening. Am I right?"

"Perhaps. This is the most important event that the people have known," said the uncle. "We don't know for sure, but it is a rare thing when the council chiefs from so many nations are called together. As you have seen, they have been gathering here with many of their people all during this moon of the budding flowers. Ever since Pathfinder returned from the mountains more and more camp fires have appeared around the lake."

"Do you know where the chiefs are going, Uncle?" asked the young man.

"It is good to see you are seeking to know," replied the uncle with a smile. "You have been named well, Fox, so I will tell you this. In our men's lodge it was told that in the great gathering a message was given to all the nations, calling the chiefs to look into a future time when the people will return. It was said that the Dreamer Chiefs from the far north have asked the elder chiefs of many nations to come to the lake of the Dreaming Islands, to travel through the obsidian mirror and see a future when the people will come again."

"What is the meaning of this, Uncle? Seeing them leave the lodge and walk so quietly into the forest and now hearing your words arouses many thoughts and feelings in me, like the white caps when the wind stirs the lake," spoke the young man intensely. "You speak of dreamers and far-away isles and an obsidian mirror and the chiefs looking into the future. I ask in respect, can you open some of these images with your words so I am not tossed about by the waves of confusion and excitement?"

"You make good sense with your words, Fox," said the uncle. "Actually, I asked you to come with me tonight because I see that one day you will make a good chief for our people. Something is beginning now, and it will be good for you to know of it. One of the important functions of a chief of the people is to look into the future and to see what is there and what will be needed. Sometimes a chief will see a short way into the future, and sometimes a chief must see a long way, like seven generations ahead. Looking this far ahead is like dreaming awake an image of that future time. The clarity of the chief's dream helps shape the future."

"You mean, what I think when I become a chief will help shape the future?" asked the young man.

"In a way yes, and in a way no," replied the uncle. "We humans have many thoughts, like the blades of grass on the prairies; so many they tangle and tumble in a huge ball sometimes. The huge drum sends out its sound and touches everything in a great circle. However, the thoughts of the chiefs I am speaking of are images so clear and bright they have a resonance that vibrates in the same way as the drum. You will have much to think on these things before your call to chieftainship comes.

"For now I want you to be aware of those you have seen going out tonight, on their journey to the Dreamer Chiefs. They will look together into the future even further than seven generations, a time when people in the future will need to seek this wisdom and will look back through time to understand the way of balance. These chiefs of the council will look together at the time when the people are ready to create a new Hoop of the people. They will look to what is needed to mend the nets in that future. Together they will lay the arrows of necessity down one by one, so our remembrance will be ready to shape that new Hoop."

"They journey forth for all of us then," responded the young man, "those we know as the people now and those we do not yet know, but who will become the people?"

"They will be the humans from many lands, the elders say; not only from this land that we know, but also from many lands across the great waters, which we have heard of. Now, Fox, let us send the chiefs we have just seen our good thoughts for their success."

The Far North

Ten trim birch bark canoes line the bank at the edge of the great northern lake. The Grandfather Sun has turned below the horizon, and the sky holds the golden pink glow, like the last sweet breath of a spring day before sleep. The smell of cedar smoke and tobacco mingle in the crisp air, as the 20 elder chiefs rise from the fire and make their way to the canoes.

Two chiefs, a man and a woman, step forward to each canoe, where they are joined by two paddlers for the bow and stern of each couple's craft. With hardly a sound the white shapes are lifted into the water, the elder chiefs settling in the center and the paddlers front and rear. At an unseen signal the 40 paddles dip into the lake, and with a gurgle the covey of craft leap forward across the smooth surface.

Line abreast, they move far out into the dark water, as light fades from the sky. At the sound of the whistle of the nightingale the canoes make a right turn to form a single line, and like an arrow with a feathered wake they move toward the north.

The night deepens the color of her cloak, and more and more of the sky dome fills with the star presence. All shoreline silhouettes have disappeared. The water is dark and depthless. Hour after hour the paddles sweep through the water in a mesmerizing rhythm, broken only by brief pauses when the paddlers rest. In one of these silent periods drifting forward, the haunting cry of the loon reaches out of the night sharpening the presence of the mystery.

They pass several small islands, some on the left, some on the right. Silent mounds of tree-covered life, the white stalks of birch trunks on the island glisten against the darker foliage. Then comes more open water, a light breeze stirring cat paws of ripples on its smooth surface.

The Dreamer Chiefs' Welcome

Finally a large island appears. It must be an hour's walk from end to end. Flickering orange-red light from a campfire at the island's center beckons, reflected in the night sky, and the canoes move silently to the birch-lined shore.

An aura of mystery surrounds them as the first canoes bearing the 20 chiefs glide toward the shore. Standing at the edge of the birch forest is an old couple, each wearing a white blanket. The old man and woman step onto the pebbled beach and catch the prows of the first two canoes and point the others to their landing spots on either side. The old man and the old woman are the Dreamer Chiefs. They are the lineage of Keepers of an ancient tradition of the people, where the power of dreaming is understood to be essential to creating a life of harmony among the people. The 20 chiefs have known of the Dreamer Chiefs and realize that the old couple will be their guides in the ceremony for which they have come.

The old man lights his pipe, sending a trail of smoke into the sky, as he gazes at a constellation. The old woman moves to each canoe and presents a small bundle to each of the elder chiefs as they step onto the shore. She steps nimbly, like someone filled with the vitality of youth. Her lined face is bright with a smile as she gently touches the hands of the visiting chiefs. The old man speaks, signing each word with his hands in fluid motion.

"We welcome each of you here and give thanks for your arrival. A warm fire is awaiting you, along with some moose meat and berries for your hunger. We will speak more of this time at the fire."

The old ones lead the way along a trail toward the fire. When they arrive and all are seated around the fire, prayers and pinches of tobacco are offered to the flames. They receive steaming bowls of food. Then the old woman speaks.

"This is a time when the people's remembrance will touch the shores of another time of the sacred dream that we call the future. The people are there now, and they are calling to us so that they can find their way again, for their memory has blurred with many journeys and distractions, and the trail of the human way has been overgrown with many new growths," she said, her face shifting and moving with the dancing flames. "We have heard their call down the spiraling trails of time and so we have summoned you."

The old man steps to the brightly burning fire and makes an offering of tobacco, tossing it into the flames. "You must feed the fire during this time," he said. "Feed it with both wood and tobacco to keep it bright during your dreaming time. Finish your meal. It will be the last food or water for the next four days and nights.

"In your dreaming journey you will visit the future that the old woman has spoken of. As council chiefs representing the nations of the people of that future time, you will bring back your insights from the dreamtime, and there will be a Wisdom Council upon your return. When we see that the people of the future are ready to renew the Hoop, we will send recommendations for their remembrance. This way the people can find their way back to the Way of the Human."

With these words, and signing, the old man hands the sack of tobacco to one of the elder women chiefs. Then he and the old woman, together with the paddlers, follow the trail back to the shore. They enter the canoes and journey to the lodge of the Dreamer Chiefs, on a nearby island.

Dreamtime Travel

The 20 chiefs sit together around the fire, ten women and ten men. Quietly they converse together looking into the fire. At the edge of the forest clearing are two large dreaming bowers made of interlaced saplings, woven tight with branches and boughs of birch, one across the fire from the other. In the firelight they dance and shimmer as the birch leaves turn in the night breeze. The cry of the loon echoes across the lake waters. After a while the women rise and go into one of the bowers to sleep, and the men enter the other bower, leaving only two to tend the fire, one man and one woman.

A deep quiet settles about the camp, broken only by an occasional snore and, once or twice, the call of a loon. As the night passes those tending the fire will be relieved at intervals by another pair, who will take their place.

The dream settles deeply about the camp, like a mist from off the lake. Definition begins to dance like the flames of the fire, and the difference between night and day blurs and melds together into one. Within the bowers the dreamers sleep deeply in the womb of the earth dream, but they share a common dream, all moving together. . .

In the dream landscape, lit only by the brilliant stars, the elder men and women chiefs wade into the waters of the lake and begin swimming down beneath the surface, gliding together like a school of sunfish. Deeper down they go, traveling together into darker water. A hint of lightness shows in the distance and grows brighter as they go deeper still. Soon the water seems to shimmer in its brightness and becomes green golden until it is as the sun seen through a veil of water. Coming through the veil and into the brightness of the noonday sun, the elder chiefs stand on the sand outside a large cave overhang.

Walking in a line, moving back into the cool recess of the cave, the chiefs come to an opening. Entering they find a large domed cavern made of bright sandstone, with incised petroglyphs on its walls and ceiling. Torches burn in niches in the walls, and the cavern has a luminous quality that dispels the darkness. A pathway of candles set in the sand leads into the center of the great dome. In this center is a large black circle, a disk of obsidian 20 paces across. It is surrounded by a rim of candles, and in its center a fire burns.

Chapter Three—*The Dreaming Ceremony* 101

The 20 chiefs divide into men and women, and the elder women chiefs take their places around the rim of the black obsidian circle while the elder men chiefs form themselves in a larger circle surrounding the women. The men chiefs sing the old welcoming song, which resonates melodiously, while the women chiefs sit in silent meditation.

When the reverberations of the men's song fall away to stillness, the two oldest women chiefs stand as Zero

Chiefs and begin to chant. Their sound is filled with beauty and longing. The others join in, making the sound whole and diverse, round and full with the many voices and strains of distant music that seems to accompany the women. They raise their voices in prayer that their vision will open and that what they see will be true. They call the wisdom doors to open, so they may see into the distant future, a time when the human family will be in need of balance. They know they must see what is to come so they can bring seeds of remembrance when the people come again.

The Women Chiefs Go Through The Obsidian Mirror

One by one, clothed only in their spirit bodies, the women chiefs travel through the shining mirror and move through the river of time. They find themselves gathered together once again, and are now able to see clearly into the world of their tomorrow, from a unique vantage point.

The beauty of the Mother Earth is breathtaking. They see Her orb moving through space. Closer and closer, as their vision expands, they see the beauty of Her oceans and mountains, and they begin to focus on the life of the many humans that people the earth. Remembering their mission to bring back a picture of the present condition of the humans living on the planet in the future, they begin to diagnose the shields of the whole human family.

Reading the East Shield

Looking through the spirit shield of the East, the women chiefs ask, "Ho, Chemah, how is the spirit fire?" They are looking for evidence of the vital force of the people, guided by the spirit of life moving through them.

In many places they see new growth, innovation, and expansion—the brightness of new creation. This is the first layer their collective vision opens. It is hopeful, and they are pleased. Now, going deeper, they look underneath the exterior. They are looking into the spirit of the people.

They see the people have become separate and many have lost their way. Many experience an absence of value and meaning, as if they have forgotten who they are and why they have come to the planet. Many are without food and work and consequently have little hope for their children's future, or their children's children. Many of the youth seek speed, thrills, and chemical ecstasy, having found no way to plant their own dreams in nourishing soil. Too many seek an early death, knowing despair to be their only companion. This is the second layer, and it brings deep concern to the ancients.

Again they expand their vision, looking deeper into the people. They are looking for hope, for inspiration, for beauty and dreams. They see these energies like fires of light on a dark night, and they are everywhere. They are found where it would be least expected. These fires of hope, inspiration and beauty are in the hearts of most of the humans alive on the planet. Each human dreams their dream, even though many have clouds covering them. They do dream. This is the third layer and possibly the most important for the ancients. This is the seed layer that awaits their coming, ready for the awakening of deep remembrance, the manifestation of dreams.

Reading the South Shield

The sounds of chanting are heard in the cosmos, ringing through the night dream. The song is one of promise. Now the women chiefs join to open the door of the South Shield and ask, "Ho, Morillah, what is the sound?" Listening to the deep sound through the water, what can be heard of the people's emotional temperament, of the deep relationship within the many peoples? The women, silent, holding, listening, begin to see.

The first layer opens to those in love, those who share beauty and joy in relationship—with spouse, children, friends, with animals and the land. They see those around the world full of laughter and friendship, seeking to expand their family circle and creating community where many voices can be heard, and the children are held in the center by all. This first layer is the sound of harmony and brings a heart-warming resonance.

The women chiefs now begin the journey to the next level, seeing underneath the surface. They open to the conflict and pain of the people, visible in many places on the Mother Earth. They see war, death, terrorism, fanaticism, vandalism, insecurity, and fear. The violence and resulting pain is crippling, the sound chaotic and dissonant. The effect on the old women is immediate. They are shocked and silent. Some appear to be struck dumb by the sounds of terror among the people, until one begins to sing. It is a song to each other, but resonates with the sound of the all. It sends a message. "We see you. We are coming. Wait for us. Look for us." Slowly, as all the voices join together, it feels as if some of the sound changes slightly, and there is a subtle change in the dissonant tempo of the people's sound.

Courage is drawn forth like a sword as the women once more open their collective vision to see the next layer. They search for the seed layer, the deepest sound in the hearts of the peoples. Through the pain and conflict they hear another sound—the sound of love. They can feel the yearning in the human family to learn how to live together once again—the yearning for peace and forgiveness, for kindness. With tears of joy the women sing their appreciation song. They rejoice, knowing the seeds are in place, kept safe within the hearts of all but a few.

Reading the West Shield

Knowing that time is critical, the women chiefs rest only moments and gather once again to open the West Shield, singing to the energy of the earth. "Ho, Ehamah, how is the body?" They look for how the container of the spirit is held, looking for balance and wellness, health and strong structure to support the growth of the many things coming into being.

As they look across the globe, they see those who remember what it means to maintain and grow structure, and they see the challenge that exists when there is so much demand. They see those who are the care givers, those who nurture and sustain that which they hold. Their vision opens to see caring enacted in individuals' lives, as people care for their children, homes, gardens, work, and crops. These are good signs, and they know there is more to see.

Expanding deeper, they open to see the energy of *being* and *becoming*. They see the majority of society focused on *becoming*—that is, doing and accomplishing. While this is powerful development, they recognize the deep well of emptiness that is not being cared for. The *being* energy—that of stillness, quiet, and contemplation—is absent to a high degree with many of the people. They know that the energy of *being*—holding and inner reflection—is crucial for the balance and wellness of a people. And this understanding enables the women chiefs to see underneath all the doing and the accomplishing, to see the stress of the lives of the people, the deep exhaustion and the sense of overwhelm. These symptoms speak of a missing inner peace and create a deep concern for the people. The women chiefs know the long-term effect of this kind of imbalance, so they begin to send a song of hope to those most affected.

And now the women approach the final layer, to see into the deepest hearts of the people. They listen underneath all the busyness, goals, and exhaustion to hear the calling. What does the human family call out for? In their vision, the women chiefs hold a bowl ready to receive the heart seeds of the people.

The seeds of yearning come one at a time, revealing the spiral deep within the heart, each one important to the well being of the human family. The first seed is *connection*. This profound calling speaks of the need to remember our connection with nature and with the spirit of oneness with all things. The second seed calling is *wisdom*, which is only possible with a deep connection to our source. The third seed reveals the calling for a sense of *global community* in which we remember how to live in peace with one another. The women chiefs hold these seeds close in their own hearts and begin their song of appreciation for what is to come.

Reading the North Shield

Reaching deeper and wider than before, the elders open the final door, that of the North Shield. Singing to the wind, the women ask, 'Ho, Wehomah, how is the breathing?' Listening to the whispers on the breeze they open the great auric envelope around the earth—Sky Girl, Sky Boy—to awaken their seeing this last time. They search for the clarity of mind and heart of the people. Testing, probing, they seek the truth, integrity, right action and courage. The wind answers with a gentle caress, carrying information of those who can walk the way of the heart.

They are able to identify those humans who are unafraid to speak the truth and admit their mistakes, who carry integrity like a banner. They see others who live a path of courage and right action, no matter how challenging. From this visioning they see the qualities of compassion and listening, honoring and respect. While there are many examples of these qualities in their vision, they are also plagued with sadness. These humans represent so few of all the human family.

As they expand their vision deeper they see the roots of the sadness. They see elements of confusion and many who live in a mind consciousness of *lack* and consider themselves victimized by those around them. They see those who rape the earth, depleting the resources that belong to all, and a terrible disparity of abundance. These forces, the women see, are fostering user attitudes and aggravating racial and cultural tensions, which erupt globally. And, maybe the most frightening, they see how many of the young people are struggling with the perceived inadequacy or irrelevance of education, leading to an unknown future with limited opportunities.

Challenged greatly, the women chiefs begin to chant, sending energy to the peoples of the earth. Their message is a mirror to what they know is the seed layer in the hearts of the people all over the earth. Hope. They sing of hope. They sing of remembrance and of the human dream. These are the seeds in the third layer, and they know they need to be awakened. The songs are calling to the seeds, saying "It is time. You are ready. Awaken now. This is the time to open, to grow your roots and to live." They sing into the night, until there is a shifting, as if the breath quickens with new life, emerging from the world of mystery with all potential opening with the dawn.

As the elder women chiefs finish the fourth song of their visioning, they sing their gratitude for all they have gathered. Then, they turn away from the vision and the incredible beauty of the Mother Earth and begin their journey back to their own time, within the cave walls and back to their dreamtime.

The Women Chiefs Return

The men chiefs sit once again with the women around the circle of the obsidian mirror. Two women chiefs and two men chiefs place themselves at the center of the circle, around the fire, to act as Zero Chiefs, who anchor the council in the protocols of the wisdom way. The other sixteen chiefs arrange themselves in pairs, one man and one woman for each of the four cardinal directions and the four marriage points in between.

One of the men Zero Chiefs stands and speaks. "We have been called to this dreamtime place as Chiefs of the Nations to look into the future. We have been asked to see into the conditions that will exist in the future and to prepare our thoughts for our Wisdom Council to send to the future.

"The women chiefs have called before us the image of the people of the future and by evoking the power of the four elementals—fire, water, earth and air—they have revealed the three levels of the collective energies of the people living then.

"What we have seen gives us a sense of gratitude and a feeling of promise, because the seeds of remembrance are still potent and alive in the people, and there is much vigor in the life of future human beings. But we have also seen grave imbalances, which affect the well-being and health of our kind and endanger the other children of the Earth Mother—the plants and animals, and even the waters, land and air. It is evident that the people have lost their way of remembering what it is to be the human, and this shows in their thoughts and actions. Perhaps this confusion has come about because so much of their attention has been focused on becoming, on the busyness of making, doing and achieving. Some way of thinking must have seized their imagination and made it prisoner, and thus they have been pulled away from the feminine energy of being. How can they be in relationship with the Great Spirit in themselves and all of life without this balance?" asks the Zero Chief.

The Mending of the Nets

"Perhaps it would be good to remind ourselves of our teaching of the mending of the nets before we look further into what these symptoms of imbalance are saying to us about this future time," continues the Zero Chief.

"The ancient symbol of the net, used to catch fish, has long been a source of teaching. The net is a simple yet sophisticated device to catch what fish are needed. It is mostly holes so it can be drawn through the water swiftly, yet has tough strands to hold the fish caught in it. By its movement not all fish are caught, and that is good, so there will always be more fish to catch. Our teaching as chiefs reminds us that we must mend our nets, for they can become torn through use. If they are not mended the fish we need will not be caught and the people will go hungry.

"From this teaching we can look into the symptoms the women chiefs have seen and perhaps determine where the nets have been torn and not mended, leaving the people not well nourished in spirit, emotion, body and mind," completes the first Zero Chief.

"In order to determine what these symptoms indicate has been torn in the nets of the people," speaks one of the women Zero Chiefs, "we recommend that the council divide into four societies to confer together: one for each of the four shields—spirit, emotion, body, and mind."

With this, the chiefs of the council agree to the first step, and the four societies gather in small circles in different parts of the cave. Each of these four circles of five chiefs reflect on the condition of one of the four shields and what these existing conditions reveal is needed to mend the nets of the people in the future.

Chapter Four
Looking Into the Shields of Humanity

The Society of the East: Shield of the Spirit

The five chiefs looking into the East Shield know that in the future there is an absence of values that guide the people in their daily lives. The society knows that this, in turn, leads to the lack of a deeper meaning in the people's lives and the sense of hopelessness to change things.

"When the fire of the spirit is not burning strong in the people how can there be a sense of deep meaning for what life is about?" asks one of the chiefs of this group. "If there is separation from the spirit of life, which is everywhere in nature, from the smallest grasses to the great star beings in the sky universe, how lonely it must be. This life energy is speaking to us all the time and in many ways. If the people cannot feel the presence of this Mystery—of the Great Spirit speaking to them, of the energy of the Mother Earth holding them, even in difficult times— how can they expect to sing their heart songs of gratitude and appreciation into each day and into the things they do?"

"We humans are sacred spirits who are part of the song of the Great Spirit of the universe," adds another chief of the East Society. "We are each a note in that song, and in our humanness we are called to seek and discover the resonance and authenticity of the sound of our spirit. And we blend its expression into the universal Mystery in the same way that birds offer their song into air, with vibrancy and without apology."

One of the women chiefs shares her thoughts. "We encourage our young to open the door of their vision from an early age. We encourage them to listen to the voice of their spirit in relation to the spirit of life and know how it will always speak to them and guide them through their journey. We teach them how to be still and listen to this spirit energy of life always, and when guided by it they will have a boundless source of hope and the vigor of the soul to express its beauty."

"From what has just been spoken we can see one of the breaks in the nets of the people of this future time," speaks a third chief of the East Society. "This hole, which needs mending, is the way of the power of the spirit within. If the people have neglected this power or shut it off from relevance in every aspect of their lives—in their self relationship, in their families, their play, their work and in creations with their groups and societies—then values, meaning and the vigor of hope naturally will diminish, like plants denied the sun. Values, meaning, and the vigor of hope are the fruits of the tree of spirit that must be nurtured in the ground of the love of the Great Spirit.

"The mending of the nets in this East Shield must begin with the people who feel the absence of spirit. These future people must council with one another on how to bring back the relationship with spirit into all that they are. They must begin to change the separation that seems to exist between the life of the spirit in them and all of their other relationships, including the work they do in groups or organizations. They must not be afraid to seek the many ways the spirit power weaves into all they think, do, and experience. There are as many ways to do this as the spring flowers in a mountain meadow. The people must once again respect diversity and honor the freedom each individual has to find the way to be truly who they are, as long as they don't hurt those they touch in relationship.

"In circles everywhere on the Mother Earth, the people of the future will need to council together on the need for spirit in their lives."

The Society of the South: Shield of Emotion

"Let us look into the condition of the nets of the people as we look at this South Shield," suggests the elder woman chief of the South Society. "Emotion is a great power in the human, but its force can harm the people or make them strong and resilient. It is a force that can make the people agile and alert if used well and guided toward appropriate responses. But if emotions are blocked or dammed, or undisciplined and indiscriminate, they reign over our actions. They can become a source of destruction of ourselves or others."

"Some of the things that we have seen as symptoms in this future time indicate the nets of the people have become torn in the way they hold the power of emotion," states one of the chiefs of the South. "When the women chiefs traveled through the obsidian mirror they saw evidence of much unresolved conflict and mindless warring, inflamed by thoughtless passion. This same excess appeared as acts of terrorism and vandalism, often among the rebellious. Widespread feelings of hesitancy and insecurity have bloomed in many places, since the power of emotion has not been channeled toward appropriate release or guided toward restorative actions."

"Emotion in the healthy human is a useful power," says another of the South Chiefs. "It arouses us to our emergent needs and stimulates us to fulfill these needs that touch the spirit, body, and mind of the individual. Emotion in the healthy human has its own needs in the cycles of experience. It weaves itself into all aspects of our relationships, shaping our feelings of well-being, like the sense of accomplishment of a difficult task, the sense of eagerness and anticipation for the new and undiscovered, or the feelings of wonder and expansion in the presence of revealing experience."

"Emotion also arouses the healthy human to alertness and readiness to action when danger is perceived, but that arousal needs to be tempered by evaluation and self-awareness," adds a fourth chief of the South Society. "The healthy human is flexible with the impact of emotional energy, able to experience the force it conveys, but neither driven by it nor indifferent to its power. The balanced and healthy human recognizes that emotional force is a call to action but not the director of action.

"For responsive actions to take place in the healthy human, either as a stimulus to fulfill needs or a call to respond to danger, a consciousness of self knowledge must be activated. This consciousness directs the stimulus or call of emotion to the heartmind. This is what we have always taught our young, that the awakened heart is the director of response. Otherwise we become prey to reaction, which is the root of thoughtlessness and violence."

Another of the chiefs continues. "What we see is that the people in this future time have somehow separated the power of emotion from its effect on their health and well being. We also see that the people are not trained in how to guide the energy of emotion to the heartmind. They need to learn to take action from the heart of clarity, which fulfills needs or responds to danger in a way that does not damage with violent energy."

A woman chief of the South Society speaks next. "Fear and anger are natural energies of the human's emotional experience. They start or startle us toward action. But dammed by inhibitions and not freely expressed or examined in a conscious way, they can fester into an outrage of destruction aimed at the self or others. And, if the only ways of expression are outrages of destruction then the societies of the people will naturally inhibit their expression and fail to examine the sources of this fear and anger.

"We need to recognize the need to mend the net in the area of emotions in this future time. First, forms and protocols of expressing fear and anger in non-violent and non-judgmental ways need to be established. These forms and protocols need to relate to all the ways in which the people come together. This must be accompanied by continuing forms of council to address these fears in regular cycles. Second, in mending the net of the South, there will need to be education on relationship and on how to establish the ground of trust at all levels, within the self and within all relationships small and large."

One of the South Society chiefs continues. "Trust cannot flower without the constant nourishing of truthful speaking and listening from the heart in a climate of respect. Mending this tear in the net must begin with all who have courage of heart, a spirit of sincerity and love for the Mother Earth. We must call ourselves and all our people to this healing in this time when we return."

The Society of the West: Shield of the Body

"As we gather here in the West Society to look into the symptoms the women chiefs have seen in the future," began an elder chief of the West Society, "we call to mind that this shield of health and well-being is the one that is focused on sustaining the life of the people. Life moves in cycles of change, and to maintain the health of the people there must be a continuing conscious attention to the balance between the *being* and *becoming* energies in the individual as well as in the people as a whole."

"What we heard from the women chiefs was a widespread emphasis on the energies of doing, of getting, making, and acquiring. These kinds of actions of accomplishment we refer to as becoming energy," adds one of the West Society chiefs.

"If we look at the people's manifestation in this future time we see an increasing sense that humans are driven by a need to pour out more and more energy to provide and expand. Less and less time is devoted to restoration and renewal, to enjoyment and reflection, and to contemplation with the mind of appreciation."

"The result of this imbalance is an absence of inner peace and harmony within many of the people, and that has given rise to conditions of high stress, overwhelm, and exhaustion," another chief of the West Society offers. "This absence threatens the sustainability of individuals as well as those forms of organization essential to the people. When we look at the need for mending the net in this area we see from these symptoms that the people must be called back to the consciousness and awareness of the laws and models of balance, which have long been part of the people's wisdom."

"When the being and becoming, the feminine and masculine energies of life are balanced, the source of life in all things in nature is renewed," adds the fourth chief of this society. "The change of seasons is an example of the balance of the feminine and the masculine. The quiet and indrawn quality of the longer nights, when the seeds of new life are dreaming, is balanced by the thrusting forth of new growth and full flowering of the longer days. For we humans these changes take place in shorter cycles, but there still needs to be a balance between the outward thrusting of making and doing and the inward restoring and renewing. This balance sustains our vigor and life."

"We see that there is a need to mend the nets of the people by restoring a focus on how to balance the circle of life energies that touch the humans in their everyday existence," continues a woman chief of the West Society. "We see that there must be an expansion of consciousness on how these life energies play a part in our well-being and help us sustain power. We humans are subject to the laws of the universe and to nature, which reflects them. We call these the Cycle of Law and the Law of Cycles, and their rhythms affect and shape all of life, including the humans and their relationships."

"In this future we see the net of consciousness of the people must be mended by an emphasis on the importance of vigilance which is part of our human heritage of wisdom," another West Chief adds. "The image of the way the healthy human moves, in balance with the energies of life, must be restored to prominence in the people's consciousness and learning cycles. This image of sustainable health of the human must include the interweaving of the energies of spirit, body, emotion, and mind in a balance and harmonious flow of relationship. This flow of relationship touches all aspects of life, both inward and outward, in all the activities of being and the actions of becoming."

The Society of the North: Shield of the Heartmind

"We are called to consider the condition of the North Shield and determine the clarity of the heart of the people in this future time," an elder chief of the North Society begins. "Confusion, a sense of lack, of being victim to disparities of abundance in the sharing of wealth, and the despoiling of Mother Earth's resources by the powerful and privileged few have been seen by the women chiefs as symptoms that impact the clarity of the heart of the people. Courage will be needed to take the necessary actions that will heal and restore these imbalances."

Another of the chiefs speaks. "We have heard from the women chiefs that the seeds of compassion and the hunger for a higher way are strong in the hearts of the people. And we are aware that the words and teachings of the many great teachers and prophets are alive in the hearts of many of the people of this coming time. All of these teachings have repeatedly called the people to a higher level of consciousness in order to respond to the needs of all the human family. We also see that many of our future people have taken responsible and courageous action in response to these teachings."

"This awareness gives a great sense of promise," speaks the third of the elder chiefs. "This sense of promise can be nourished in the future time by calling all the people of good heart to come together in circles to share what is needed to respond to the symptoms the women chiefs saw in this North Shield. The widespread despoiling of nature and a huge disparity of abundance between the different members of the human family would indicate that there is wide separation among these future people, from one another and from the natural world they live with. With such separation the heart of knowing and compassion will easily close, for it becomes hard to feel what it is like to walk in another's moccasins or cherish the presence of nature."

"The petty consciousness that arises out of unexamined fear and the people's sense of lack cuts off the opening of the heartmind energy, like covering the flame of a torch with a blanket. In such a smothering atmosphere there arises a grasping urgency, and that grasping leads to short-sighted and unconscious attitudes in relationship, like exploitation and control. These attitudes separate the people from one another," offers one of the women chiefs.

"The heart of the people must open to a higher consciousness for them to care for one another and rise above separations and difference. This higher consciousness is characterized in individuals and groups by a strong and caring heart, which is concerned for the well-being of all our human family and all our relations in nature," adds another of the chiefs. "The fears and sense of lack that have been spoken of will be transformed in the atmosphere of the strong and caring hearts of the people."

"Meaningful education for the young in developing their higher consciousness will prepare them to assist in shaping a new culture of awareness, so that the people understand their relationship with the Mother Earth and all her children, including their fellow humans. Circles of people can support each other in developing their group skills of higher consciousness and in raising individual levels. This will help create a higher collective consciousness, which will spread out and help open the heart of courage among all the people," completed the fifth elder chief of the North Society.

"We see then, from our sharing, that a high priority in mending the net at this Shield of the North is to make clear the need to awaken a higher level of collective consciousness among all the people," spoke the first of the elder chiefs of this society.

"It is as you have spoken," the other four chiefs concurred.

The Council Question

When the four societies of chiefs had completed their considerations about the mending of the nets, a soft drumming called the chiefs back to their seats at the obsidian mirror. In silence the sacred pipe was passed from chief to chief as each breathed visible prayers of smoke upward into the cavern.

Then, one by one, each society reported on what they had seen in their reflections, stating what was needed to mend the nets for each of the four shields. The image grew in the minds of each chief of a strong, restored net of consciousness sent to the people of the future, assisting them and providing nourishment, healing the imbalances of that future world.

"When we all reflect on the significance of these four areas where the net of consciousness needs to be mended, we see the image of the people becoming strong again as they begin the mending," states the Zero Chief of the West.

The Zero Chief of the East speaks. "We see in this future time the message spreading that there is the awakening of spirit amongst the people in all of their groups and organizations. We can see the restoring of evocative leadership, calling the people to awaken the spirit of a new mind of consciousness of the universe of possibility. We see being enacted in that time the forms and protocols to explore and address the fears and issues of lack among the people in a caring and responsive way. We see the exposition and teaching of models of balance flowing out amongst the people and also a widespread call to higher consciousness arising in all the lands where the people dwell on the Mother Earth."

"From this seeing that we are holding as chiefs, a question comes to us that we are called to take to our Wisdom Council. We will gather our responses to this question and our recommendations to the people of this future time. The question we are called to consider in our council is: *What are the primary actions needed to awaken and manifest the promise of the heart seeds in the hearts of the people that will allow them to return their world to balance?* We will contemplate this question as council chiefs and prepare for the Wisdom Council," finished the Zero Chief of the South.

The Zero Chief of the North begins a song of welcome, calling the Great Spirit to be with the chiefs in their contemplation so they can hold the well-being of all the people in this future time. Together the chiefs call for the deepest source of wisdom revealed in the dreamtime to prepare them for when they are called by the Dreamer Chiefs for the Wisdom Council.

Chapter Five
The Transmission

The Dreamer Chiefs

After the Old Man and Old Woman Dreamer Chiefs had left the dreaming circle of chiefs, having offered them their last food for four days and nights, they returned to their village, an island away. There they began a dreaming vigil of their own, in which they prayed for the Chiefs of the Nations and the work they were doing. Each day they offered their morning prayers to the fire outside their lodge and then entered their own dreaming state in which they could see the chiefs and experience their travels and insights, as if present in the dreamtime with them.

Looking at the Old Man was like seeing the nobility of an ancient tree. He had a deeply lined face and eyes like dark pools. When moving he was fluid and quick, like the deer, belying his 78 years of living on the earth. His skin was a soft brown color, and he wore moccasins up to his calf and close fitting leather clothes. His dark and graying hair was woven into two braids, hanging down his chest.

The Old Woman carried a peaceful smile, consistent with the sense of peace behind her eyes. She had a fullness about her, and with an ample gracefulness her whole being moved fluidly. Whether she sat still working on her beading, or was sharing a story or cooking, she appeared to be rooted, as if deeply anchored to the earth. Shorter than the Old Man by an open hand, she too had graying hair braided about her beautiful face. Her dress hung simply to her ankles, the bodice woven with intertwining flowers.

The Old Man and the Old Woman were at their fire where they had been accompanying the dreaming chiefs in the dreamtime. The task of adding wood to the fire was held by the Old Man, as he deeply connected with his prayer through the fire. The Old Woman continued her practice of adding tobacco to the fire with her prayer, much the same as it had been in these last days and nights by these old ones, in deep concert with the Chiefs of the Nations.

They spoke to each other now in quiet, intimate tones, still very present in both worlds.

"I see they have come through a doorway," spoke the Old Man. "The learning has been deep. Soon they will be ready to emerge from their dreamtime journey. They have shared many insights and have brought back a profound seeing of the future through the mirror."

"Soon we must prepare their welcoming feast and greet them," spoke the Old Woman.

The Dreamer Chiefs each offered prayers of gratitude to the sacredness of life for this ceremony time and began their preparations.

Awakening From the Dreamtime

In the pre-dawn silence the mist lifts from the island. In the two dreaming bowers there is a stirring as the men and women chiefs rouse from their Dreamtime sleep. Another couple, tending the fire, add fresh wood and listen to the comforting crackles.

Thus, the Chiefs of the Nations find themselves awakening on the morning of the fifth day. Stretching, the women open their eyes to the morning sky, so different from the energy of the cave in the dreamtime. The early morning light is chasing away the darkness of the night sky, and the birds are calling them to rise. Emerging from the dreaming bower, the women marvel at the passage of time and recognize they have learned much in this time of dreaming. The men meet them at the fire, and they offer morning prayers together. Each is deeply touched by the experiences of the dreamtime and hold in their conscious memory all that they saw, shared and contemplated. They greet each other knowing that this day they will sit in council.

"Ho, the Dreamer Chiefs approach, welcome to our fire," one of the women chiefs says.

They watch the Old Man and the Old Woman walk into the circle, each carrying baskets full of berries, moose meat and fresh greens. After fasting for four days and nights the people's bodies and spirits are especially ready for this welcoming feast. Special herb tea is prepared and offered, the first drink after these dreaming days and nights.

Soon there was a fullness of energy in the stomachs of each of the chiefs as they sat sharing quiet words by the fire, each of them gazing at the birch trees that had held them during their ceremony. The air was crisp, and everything seemed crystalline and fresh, as if they had just been born into a new life.

Having eaten their meal, the Chiefs of the Nations gather to listen to the old Dreamer Chiefs in preparation for the council. The Old Woman spoke first.

"We have felt you in your dreaming time and know you have journeyed far and have brought back great wisdom. Soon you will sit in council. The substance of that council will be sent as a transmission to the future time. When we come again as the people of the future you have visited, the memory of this Wisdom Council must be imprinted in the seeds you have seen in the minds and hearts of that time.

"In the future the energy of the collective consciousness has been largely forgotten in the increasing isolation that surrounds humans at that time," spoke the Old Man. "Until those people restore their sense of belonging together as tribal groups, the individual's memory and access to inherent wisdom will be diminished by this lack of collective identity.

"We will follow the Wisdom Council with a ceremony. In the ceremony we will invoke the energies of our collective intelligence, surrounding the event of the council like an aura, and through the power of our prayer we will send the substance of this council to the realm of the collective consciousness of all human memory cells of this future time," explained the Old Woman Dreamer Chief.

As these words were spoken a mist drifted in from the lake, enveloping the island and the chiefs in a mantle of mystery. As the Chiefs of the Nations made their preparations for council, sounds of distant thunder rolled through the stillness. Each was aware of the portent of this time and the power of change and transformation the thunder beings signaled. One by one the loaded canoes of the chiefs slipped into the water of the lake, traveling to a nearby island where many of the people were gathered for the Wisdom Council.

The Wisdom Council

Because of the call that went out, representatives of many tribes have gathered for the Wisdom Council in a lovely high meadow overlooking a great lake. Surrounding the meadow, and making a background for the many lodges of the representatives, stands a forest of tall sentinel pine trees. They provide an energy of purity and give eloquent dignity to the setting.

At the sound of a deep drumming rhythm, the Chiefs of the Nations move in a column of pairs, making their way through the gathered throng of representatives and into the council circle, which is defined by eight tall poles spaced around the perimeter. On each of these poles is mounted a large painted shield, depicting in design the different symbols of each of eight different elemental perspectives, which will be represented by two chiefs, male and female, during the council.

Entering the council circle, the eight pairs take their place in the council, a pair at each of the eight poles. In the center the two pairs of remaining chiefs take their places as Zero Chiefs at the four cardinal points around the center fire, called the Children's Fire. All 20 chiefs are dressed in beautiful garments made of the soft, light, tanned deer skin, fringed at arms and legs and adorned with intricate designs of beads and quills. Eagle feathers, hanging from the braided hair of the chiefs, move gently in the morning breeze from the lake.

The drumming stops. The sound and shadow of a large flock of geese flying north passes over the meadow. Grasses rustle in the meadow, blown by breezes from the lake. Crows settle noisily into the branches of one of the tallest pines. The smell of smoke from the Children's Fire perfumes the air. The morning sun warms the skin of people. Colors are bright on the many banners and blankets. A sense of quiet anticipation is dominant throughout the meadow.

The vibrant rising note of a woman's voice lifts skyward, followed by a chorus of hundreds of voices, blending in a harmony. They are singing a prayer of gratitude to life and it ripples in waves across the meadow and then ends abruptly, as one voice into silence.

A crier, carrying a long staff enters the circle and announces in a strong voice, "This Council of Chiefs from The Many Nations has now assembled. We call out the question: *What are the primary actions needed to awaken and manifest the promise of the heart seeds in the hearts of the people that will allow them to return their world to balance?* Let this council of wisdom for the future now begin!"

At this, the chiefs seat themselves on the woven willow mats with back rests, positioned at each of their places. Only the two chiefs at the East gate of the circle remain standing. The woman chief holds the long staff given to her by the crier. After a moment of silence she begins to speak in a loud clear voice that reaches the farthest ear of the circle of representatives.

"As you are all aware, we are gathered here to listen to the recommendations of this council of chiefs to be sent to the future. We have listened to all your voices in our dreaming time of contemplation on the question that has come forward to this Wisdom Council.

"We begin with the awareness that this council speaks as one voice, but with eight different perspectives. The one voice from which we each speak is informed by the spirit that guides us now, the same spirit of life that will guide us in the future time we now consider."

As the words from the woman chief ring out to the ears of the people a subtle shift of energy pervades the meadow. There is a stillness, an anticipation, present. It is as if every blade of grass, every tree, is part of that stillness.

Into this stillness the words of the eight pairs of chiefs ring out one by one in a rich tapestry of poetic sound. A design is woven of thoughtful recommendations that grew from their considerations in the cave of the dreamtime.

The eloquence of these thoughts, spoken by the chiefs, touches the hearts of the assembled people, and a collective prayer of blessing to the future is voiced when the last of the chiefs has spoken.

The large ceremony drum is sounded. The council is complete.

Before leaving the council circle, speeches are heard from several of the representatives of the people. They bring words of gratitude to the Chiefs of the Nations. Then the chiefs leave the council circle as they entered, in respect for the energy of life that has supported their journey.

Ceremony of Transmission

Recognizing the vital importance of their final task, the chiefs prepare for the last part of their time together: the Ceremony of Transmission. Each of them knows the power of thought and how our energy consciousness is connected through space and time.

Once more they enter their canoes and take themselves back to the dreaming island. Arriving, they pass the bowers of their dreaming ceremony as the dusky evening beckons them into the depth of the birch forest. They hear the wind whispering in the trees and know the spirits are gathering.

The Dreamer Chiefs call the spirits with the song of the flute. One by one the guardians appear as if by magic, coming from the circle of trees. They are the Guardian Spirits of the Sacred Hoop of the people. They appear only when their special gifts are needed. Now they are being called to carry the message of this council into the future.

The Old Man and the Old Woman Dreamer Chiefs stand together by the fire in the center of the circle. The Old Woman's song, carried by the wind, touches the tops of the ancient birch trees surrounding the fire. The song seems to dance with the smoke from the Old Man's pipe as he offers prayers to the spirit of the grandmothers and the grandfathers.

The Chiefs of The Nations sit in contemplation around the fire, each holding the intention for the awakening of remembrance in the future generations. They pray for the heart seeds, the deepest dreams in the hearts of the people to open. They pray for the remembrance of the sacredness of life, and for the deepest yearning in the hearts of the people to come awake. They ask the Guardian Spirits to carry their prayers and messages of hope into the future. Each of the chiefs sits in the circle while the spirits of the guardians dance to the sound of the spirit drum. They feel the power of the spirit dance and know the message of remembrance will be carried.

Discerning eyes see the spirit guardians move away and disappear into the forest. They carry the message forward in time, where it once more will be heard on the wind.

The message is for all the people, not only a few. Every heart carries the seeds of remembrance. Soon it will be time for the seeds to open. As the last of the old ones disappear into the trees, the song of the Old Woman comes to an end.

the Present

We are called to awaken.
We are called.
Listen now, listen!
It is in the whisper on the wind.
There is a presence.
It is all around us.
Calling us.
To awaken.

WindEagle (2003)

part Three
Awakening and Remembering

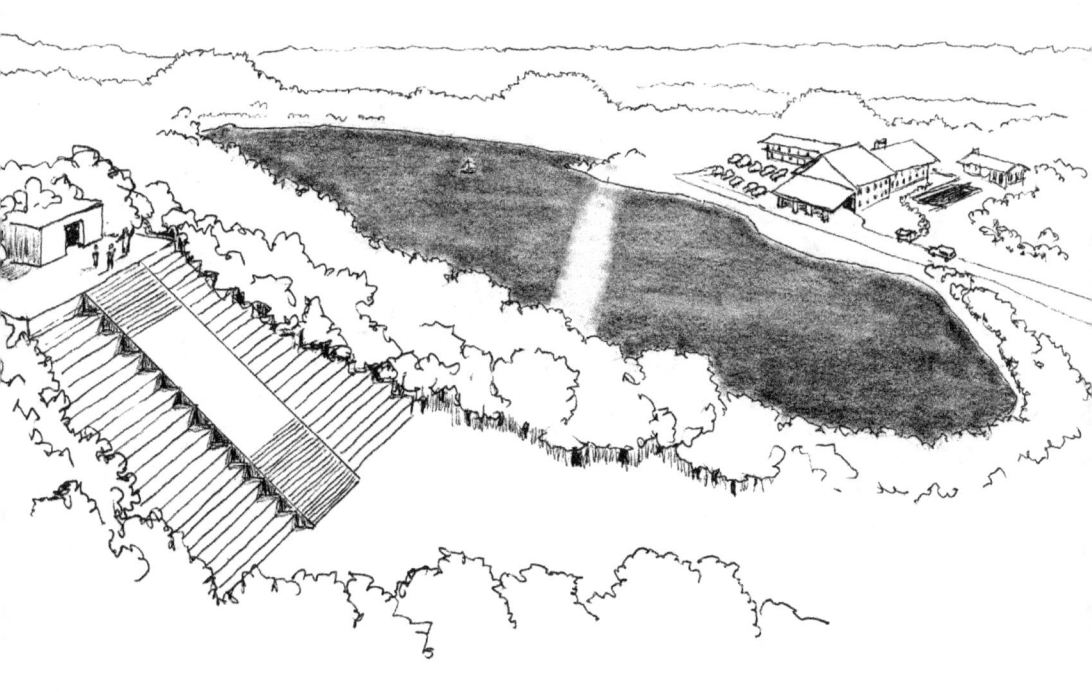

Chapter Six
The Call to the North

The Heart Seeds Call

Willow awakened from the dream with a start, feeling propelled back into a reality she didn't recognize. Slowly, opening her eyes, she remembered where she was. Falcon, her husband, lay beside her in the hotel suite. He was still sleeping, which was good. Normally he was up first, having coffee, smoking his pipe, and getting a head start on the day. The sun wasn't up yet so she lay back, savoring these early moments alone with her thoughts. The meeting, she knew, wouldn't start until the next day, so she had plenty of time.

This was their first time in Quintana Roo and the third, or was it the fourth, time together with this group of business people. Senior-level executives from several companies, they came together four times a year to learn from each other and inquire into the newest technology or knowledge wave that could help them and their companies be more successful. Most of them had been meeting for so many years they had become like a family. They actually were a highly unusual group, because their primary purpose for meeting was to learn from one another.

As she stretched and turned over, Willow reviewed the state of her life and did her usual morning practice of checking in. Grateful for the many years of seeking and training to be a medicine keeper of the old wisdom, she spent time sending prayers of gratitude to her teachers. They seemed close these days, like a presence around her, continuing to guide and teach her. Her appreciation of her life, her sacred work, her health, her family seemed to expand like waves of light as she sent out her morning prayers. She rose and danced the Tslagi, an ancient Cherokee dance of healing, in front of the hotel-room altar she had created the night before.

Willow sometimes found it challenging to pray inside a hotel. It was so much easier to be connected with the Sacred Source on top of a mountain or in the desert. But today was different. Maybe it was something from her dream. She wished she could remember it, but all she could recall was a sense of urgency.

Turning around, she realized Falcon was up and dressed and ready to explore the hotel grounds. Hurrying to dress she called out "Let's meet at the water," and she disappeared into the dressing room.

Falcon sipped his coffee and ruminated while he loaded his pipe. He was taking in the beauty of the land in the gardens surrounding the building and tracing the lineage of the old wisdom ways he and Willow carried. The old stories of Flys Crow and Temple Doors, ancient Keepers of the Medicine, were fresh in his mind. Maybe they actually traveled here centuries ago. Deeply touched by being in proximity with the ancient Mayan temples, the origins of the Ancient Way, Falcon offered his prayers to Life through his pipe. As always he sent his thanks to the Great Mystery for his life, the joy of his sacred partnership with Willow, and for the opportunity to once again share the old wisdom.

Chapter Six—The Call to the North

Breaking him out of his reverie, he felt Willow's hand on his shoulder, just a light touch, indicating so much gentleness, caring, and love. His heart expanded, and he placed his hand on hers. Both approaching their 60s, they still shared a strong spirit of adventure.

The humid tropical air kept the trees and plants in constant motion as they walked hand in hand, exploring the gardens surrounding them. Waves thundered behind them, crashing on the outcroppings of volcanic rock. Suddenly the wind dropped, and all the plants seemed to come to rest.

Willow found herself looking up at a very large tree. She noticed small leaves or insects falling and dipping, turning and landing at her feet. Picking one up, she saw it was a seed from the tree, in the shape of a heart. All around the seed itself was a clear membrane, almost like cellophane. She marveled at its beauty. As she held the seed in her hand she suddenly realized what she was looking at. She remembered her dream, and her pulse began to race as the sense of urgency from the dream once more surged within her. She called Falcon to join her there, under the tree, and soon found herself sharing her dream.

"You and I were walking here in the Yucatan, in the jungle, searching for the moon temple. We needed to be there for the full moon. There was to be a ceremony of remembrance," she said.

Falcon listened, holding both her hands tightly, as filled with awe and wonder as Willow was. She continued.

"We found the base of the temple, and just as we approached it a mist completely enveloped us and the temple. We couldn't see anything. Then there was an old man who looked like a Mayan priest. We heard him speaking to us. He described a tree with heart seeds. 'These seeds will be a sign of the return,' he said. It was so vivid. That's all I can remember. Oh, except it was urgent that we find them. What do you think it means?"

Falcon took one of the seeds, contemplated it, and said "Let's walk down to the water, spend some time there, and see what comes to us."

They enjoyed the beautiful turquoise water and powdery white sand. The day went quickly, but by the end of the day they had no more answers than when they began. They decided to hold the question: What do the heart-shaped seeds signify?

This was a medicine practice they found extremely useful. It simply meant they would remember, or "hold" the question but not try to answer it. It was a little bit like putting the question into an open basket and carrying it with you, not pursuing an answer, just being receptive. They both knew that receiving an important dream with a message to find a tree with heart seeds, and the same morning to actually find the tree, was a very important medicine sign. Now they would wait, open and alert to what Life says is the next step.

At the Conference in Mexico

The first day of the conference took them to Coba, an ancient Mayan pyramid. The jungle had completely covered all the buildings since the Mayans had abandoned it. And even now, since its discovery over 30 years ago, it was only halfway uncovered.

Falcon and Willow offered some opening thoughts for the group about how to view the site. "Imagine each of you live in this ancient time. You are a part of the culture and have been a part of creating what you see. See it as yours. It belongs to you. Now, from that perspective, ask yourself what you do here. Who are you and what is your relationship with this place? Look from the inside and access your own knowing about this ancient place. Hold these thoughts as we journey today. This afternoon we will speak of who we are in this society."

In the early afternoon, following lunch, the group gathered in a place where they could all sit together, on the bottom steps of the pyramid. One by one they began to introduce themselves, as residents of the ancient Mayan community. While all of them felt the excitement and play coming from their imagination, they also sensed a deeper current of truth within each other's words.

As each one spoke the images and stories grew. Slowly a tapestry was created in which could be seen a very real culture of the long distant past. There were artisans, politicians, masons, and astronomers. Willow stood to say she had been a Mayan priestess named Flys Crow who advised the ruler, her sister, in how to bring balance to the energies of the masculine and feminine. Falcon stood beside her then, as now. He remembered himself to be a Mayan Priest, advisor to the high council, with the name of Ocean Bow.

Later that night, back at the hotel, Willow and Falcon spoke of the synchronicity of Willow's dream, speaking of the "return." They smiled as they imagined themselves as Flys Crow and Ocean Bow.

The next meeting days were held indoors, with speakers and group discussions. On the last day the people gathered and spoke their appreciation for their time together. They used an old wisdom practice called *stringing the beads*.

Each one spoke in their own way of how the time had impacted them and what they took away with them. They all recognized that they had touched the magic of the land and felt their relationships deepen through their experience together.

At the Pyramid

After the conference ended Falcon could no longer ignore the strong feeling that had been nagging him all day. He was being pulled to go back to Coba, and he finally spoke to Willow about it. As Willow listened she sensed the importance of going back to the pyramid. They agreed to return that same night and do a medicine-pipe ceremony.

They prepared themselves carefully, as they knew unseen forces were drawing them forward and they needed to be alert. Saying many prayers, they both dressed in their ceremonial clothing. They prepared a special offering of tobacco, sage, sweetgrass, and copal resin for the ancestor spirits of this land and set out for the temple pyramid.

Dusk brought the evening shadows as they approached the ancient site. Several birds were making themselves known with their warbling music, and in the distance they caught sight of a monkey ascending a tree. The sky was magnificent this evening, glowing with brilliant reds and oranges. Everything seemed to shimmer as they made their way slowly to the top of the pyramid.

Falcon reached the top of the pyramid first and had set the blanket and their altar items in preparation. He extended a hand to Willow, who was climbing the last few steps. The night became silent as they began a chant, sending their voices into the night sky, calling to the spirits to receive their offerings.

"We come in respect of the ancestors," they sang. "We come in a good way. Hear us, Grandmothers. Hear us, Grandfathers. Hear our prayer."

They offered their pipes to the old ones and sent their visible breath to the Great Mystery, calling for the healing of the Sacred Hoop of the people. Sitting in quiet contemplation, Falcon looked at Willow and saw movement behind her. Not sure if his eyes were seeing clearly, he nevertheless kept his gaze focused just beyond her left shoulder. The figure he saw was definitely feminine and seemed to be real, yet his logical mind could not understand where she came from.

He shifted his gaze quickly to signal Willow, but she already had felt the presence and moved to join him. They both rose and turned to meet what looked to be a Mayan priestess.

Her skin was beautiful, a luminescent copper color. She wore a headdress decorated with silver and many long blue quetzal feathers. Her dress came to her ankles, and she wore sandals on her feet. Around her neck she wore a gold jaguar-shaped medallion surrounded by turquoise. They listened closely as she spoke, her words seeming to come from a great distance. As they looked into her face, it was as if they were held suspended in time. Her eyes, like deep green pools, called them into the shimmering.

"You have been here before. It is good you have come again. This is the temple of your ancestors.

"We have called you here to receive our message. This is a time of great change. The ancient ones prophesied this as the ending time of a 5000-year cycle, knowing the potential now exists to open the door to a new manifestation of the human spirit.

"It is imperative you realize you have a responsibility now, in this time of the turning. You must understand your role. This is a time of great potential and calls for heightened awareness. You are meant to play a part in this shifting of consciousness.

"Hear me. You must travel to the far north to find the Old Man and the Old Woman. Go to the Dreamers. They carry the knowledge of the people's return. Find them."

Both Falcon and Willow bowed as the Priestess disappeared into the night. Just as her vision faded they heard the cry of the jaguar and a strong gust of wind swirled around them. They offered silent prayers of thanksgiving for the honor of her visit. Willow and Falcon both were silent for some time, feeling challenged by the power of her message.

They also took time to remember, together, each word of the message they had been given. When they were finished the sky was pitch black and filled with stars. The moon had risen. They gathered their altar materials and pipe bags and began to make their way carefully down the steps of the pyramid. The steps were very steep, so they moved slowly in a rhythmical dance, first he, then she, flowing like a waterfall cascading down a rocky mountain.

Early the next morning Falcon woke Willow and asked her to walk on the beach. They both were very full with their experience of the night before and silently approached the water. Then Falcon spoke.

"Willow, you know we have both felt this coming, and I feel we need to give this a priority in our lives. I know we have lots of training groups and ceremonies coming up, but I feel it is imperative we follow the instructions we've been given and see the Dreamer Chiefs as soon as possible."

Willow nodded in agreement as she listened, and Falcon spoke again.

"We both know this is a very important time of change in the world and that we have a part to play in that change. Many others do as well. But we really need to do this. What do you feel about this Willow?"

She took his arm and wove hers through his, as she often did, and started them walking again. "First of all, Falcon, I am honored, and I'm feeling a deep sense of responsibility. I have waited a long time for this to come. Now that it is here, I am in awe. There is much to do to bring a shift of consciousness on this planet and to create a culture of peace. I know my dream, and this message is connected. I am willing to do whatever we can to be a part of this work, along with many others. We need to make plans right away. How soon do you think we can manage it?"

Going North

The twin engine, propeller-driven monoplane roared northward over the seemingly endless forests and jewel-like lakes of northeastern Canada. The man and woman sat together in two forward seats of the small cabin looking out the window at the vast green carpet of life below them.

"How beautiful the northern earth is," said Falcon. "It is amazing to think that only one week ago we were in the midst of her jungles and palm trees of Quintana Roo in Mexico, and now we are approaching the Arctic Circle just west of the Hudson Bay!"

"Yes, and I am struck by this beautiful green mantle of her growing life, so different and yet so similar in its vibrance," responded the beautiful woman beside him. Willow's flowing auburn and silver hair was drawn back in a long braid, and her bright eyes shone with joy beneath her visor cap. "This is the land where Tomasiasah, the Cree medicine woman, came from isn't it?"

"That's right," replied Falcon, "and this is the country where she trained the young Eschima over one hundred years ago."

They were referring to two legendary carriers of the old teaching belts, one of which was given to Tomasiasah during the great tribal gathering in Oklahoma in 1879, when the tribes of North America were facing the final onslaught of Europe's massive immigration to the Americas. At this gathering, the remaining teaching belts, which carried the wisdom designs of the indigenous cultures, were given to 37 medicine women to carry. The men were called to fight in the terrible battles of extinction that were pressed against them by the armies of the rapidly-expanding country of the United States.

"I can imagine Tomasiasah walking through those forests below with young Eschima teaching her the medicine ways from nature," said Willow. "See the winding trail leading from that group of cabins," she said, pointing. "It must have been like this when they walked the land."

Steve and his wife Diane, along with two other couples, Bran and Katherine and Kurt and Eva, were accompanying Falcon and Willow on this journey to meet the Dreamer Chiefs. They had come together from different places in the world. Steve and Diane were from opposite sides of the United States, Kurt and Eva from Germany and Austria, and Bran and Katherine from the United Kingdom. All of them had been studying to be medicine teachers with Willow and Falcon for several years and were part of the training staff of the California institute that Willow and Falcon established in 1987. They were like a family now. Through a kind of magic they had grown familiar with, each of the couple's lives had changed as they were called by a yearning to search for deeper meaning in the way they lived.

After the encounter with the priestess of the Mayan temple and her words of instruction to them, Willow and Falcon decided they should take these advanced students of the Medicine Way with them to meet the Dreamer Chiefs. It seemed wise to have more eyes and ears to take in the Dreamer Chiefs' message.

At that moment the co-pilot leaned into the cabin and signaled, pointing at his watch and holding up the fingers of both hands to indicate they would be landing in ten minutes. Steve then leaned forward from his seat, behind Falcon and Willow.

"We're going to land down there?" he asked. "I don't see anything but trees and those lakes, and I don't remember seeing any pontoons when we climbed aboard this crate. These guys must have eyes like eagles if they see some place to land!"

"Look," cried Diane, pointing out the other window. "There's a village at the edge of the lake over there, and I can see what looks like a small runway a short distance to the right."

"My gosh!" exclaimed Steve. "You've got eyes like an eagle too!"

Everyone started clapping as the small plane banked to the right and started down over the forest trees toward the small dirt runway. The pilot brought the plane in for a smooth landing and taxied across the field to a small building with corrugated walls and roof. As soon as the engine shut down the co-pilot opened the cabin door.

"Here we are folks. Have a good time," he said with a smile, and he started to throw their backpacks out the door.

Arrival and Greeting in the Land of the Dreamers

As they climbed down and stretched, Bran asked, "How are we supposed to get our stuff to wherever we're going? I don't see any trucks or taxis. Not even a car!"

"I think we're going to walk," said Falcon. "That's the way they do it up here, so put on your backpacks and we'll follow that trail over there by the building. It leads to the lake, where someone will meet us."

The next moment the plane engine roared to life, and the group watched as the pilot waved and the plane rolled off, lifting into the sky and disappearing beyond the tall ring of pine trees which surrounded the runway. A deep and soothing silence surrounded the small group as the sound of the departing plane died out. Only a soft soughing of the breeze through the lovely pine boughs was heard.

Finally Eva spoke the word "schönheit," meaning "beauty" in German.

"It is as if time has stopped in this moment of beauty," she said as she raised her graceful arms to the sky.

"In a way it is true," said Willow. "We are stepping through a shimmering door in our journey together where we sense time has taken on another dimension."

Each one shouldered their packs, and they began to walk on the trail, with only the soft sound of needles beneath their feet. After walking for nearly an hour, Willow, Falcon and their group emerged from the forest at the edge of a lake of deep blue water. The afternoon sun sparkled on the small wavelets, and far down the curving beach a motorboat sped out from a small village of houses and turned in their direction.

"Looks as if Stan knows we've arrived," said Falcon, pointing.

"Stan is the Cree Indian we told you about who we met when we came here twelve years ago," said Willow. "He's a wonderful spirit, and so is his wife Susan. You'll love them both."

Falcon and Willow had both visited the Dreamer Chiefs years ago as part of their journey of taking on the responsibility of being keepers of the Delicate Lodge. The Delicate Lodge is the body of the ancient wisdom way of the medicine that was the foundation of the indigenous culture of the Americas. At that time Stan Morrisen and his wife Susan had greeted them and prepared them for their time with the old Dreamer Chiefs.

Part of their preparation was the experience of the couple's hospitality, the good food, many stories and wonderful laughter. They carried the essence of the Cree people of this region, whose people hunted the moose, fished the lakes, and cared for one another in the old tribal ways of interdependent family clans.

As the motorboat hit the shore, Stan stood up and leaped onto the sand beach. He was a large bronzed-skinned man with a bear-like body, long black braids and a generous smile.

"Well I see you have arrived with some of your clan this time," laughed Stan. "Must be something big coming up, eh?"

Stan clasped Willow and Falcon with a big hug and then gave the others a smile, saying a word of welcome to each. "We had a message from the island that you might be coming, and then we got your letter last week, making it a sure thing. Susan has prepared a meal of moose and berries, which Falcon and Willow liked so much the last time, so you won't go hungry," Stan said, smiling. "Come on, throw your packs in the boat and I'll run you to the cabin."

With laughter and joking, everyone loaded on board, and Stan gave the boat a shove off the shore, jumped in, and sat in the stern. With a flick of his big hand he pulled the cord of the large outboard engine, and it roared into a solid rhythm. Stan maneuvered the boat around, and they sped off, the bow spray flinging past them.

As the party approached the cabin they saw Susan standing in the doorway, with a baby on one hip and two older children peering around her at the visitors. Susan was a tall, lithe woman with almond skin and beautiful dark eyes. Her hair, loosely tied, hung below her waist, and she wore a white deerskin hide dress decorated with beaded designs.

Susan came down the steps of the cabin and moved to greet Willow and Falcon with a warm embrace. She shook hands with each of the others. "Come inside," she said smiling, "I have food ready for you. I thought you would be hungry after the long flight on our 'northern woods airlines.'"

Falcon and Willow knew from experience that the openness and security of a warm welcome was part of the greeting ritual, which was the beginning of their journey to the Dreamer Chiefs. They both knew that Stan and Susan, medicine people in their tribe, were part of a tightly woven fabric of tribal consciousness. Stan and Susan were closely connected with the Dreamer Chiefs, and with their welcoming offering they were preparing the way for the group's time with the Old Man and Old Woman Dreamer Chiefs. Before their arrival Falcon and Willow had advised each of their group of this old tribal custom and cautioned them to be respectful and also mindful.

"It's been a long time," Stan said, raising his glass of juice after they sat down. "You have a bigger family now, and as you can see, so do we." Stan looked at the faces of their son and two daughters, who were looking shyly at the newcomers, before he continued.

"Let's each speak our names and a word or two as we begin our meal. That way Mother Earth will know who's partaking of her giveaway," suggested Susan.

So the feasting began with stories and laughter, with each person sharing in the warm welcome energy of being together. Throughout the evening more stories were shared, telling of each of their journeys. Susan and Stan listened well and shared their past adventures also. In this environment it was easy to feel at home.

After a restful night the group was awakened by Stan and given a hearty breakfast at Susan's table. No mention was made of their visit to the Dreamer Chiefs, except Stan said that their boat would arrive in the afternoon. During the morning everyone helped with various chores, and later the men went out with Stan in the boat to fish. The women gathered out behind the cabin with Susan and talked together while baking bread loaves in her brick oven.

When the men returned they cleaned the catch of fish and packed them with ice in a foam chest. The women brought in the sweet smelling loaves of warm bread and wrapped them in bright colored cloths. The group shared their morning experiences with each other while they lunched on sandwiches and iced tea.

The mood was one of anticipation, as the group knew the time was approaching for the journey to the island where the Dreamer Chiefs lived. Stan showed them the maps of the large lake and the island they were going to. "It's about a four-hour trip by motorboat," he said. "The weather is calm today so you'll have a smooth ride."

"If you keep your eyes open, you may see some moose at the water's edge as you pass the big islands on the other side, over here," said Susan, drawing the tip of a feather across the map. "It will be dusk by then and they like to come to the water to drink at that time."

"I'd sure like to see one," Kurt said. "Maybe even get a picture. You know, I can still feel the energy from that wonderful meal of moose and berries you gave us last night."

Chapter Six—The Call to the North

"We'll probably get to taste some more when we're with the Old Man," said Falcon. "He is known to be a great hunter, even though he is in his 80s. When Willow and I were here before he kept us filled with that energy. He said that moose meat is good for dreaming."

After lunch everyone packed their gear, and Stan came and told them to take their packs down to the dock in preparation for leaving. Soon a boat appeared in the distance, a lone figure at the tiller. Everyone stood up and watched its approach.

"It's the Old Man. He has come to get us himself," said Willow waving and smiling. The figure in the boat waved back, and a few moments later the smiling face of the Old Man looked up from beside the dock.

"It is good you have come back now," he said to Falcon and Willow. "Tell your people to put their things in the boat. We will leave right away," he said, pointing across the lake.

Stan and Susan handed the chest of fish and the wrapped loaves of bread down into the hands of the Old Man. He neatly stowed them beneath his seat in the stern. Together the three spoke some words quietly, in Cree, and then touched hands together.

"All right, off you go," Stan said to the eight travelers.

"Good medicine. We'll be waiting for your safe return," Susan added.

As the couples climbed in their seats Susan took Willow's hand, and they looked into each other's eyes. "We know you have been called to an important time," she said. "We will hold you all in our prayers."

Willow nodded, smiled, and climbed into the boat. Stan gave Falcon one of his hugs and a slap on the back, and then Falcon climbed aboard. The Old Man gunned the outboard and turned the craft out into the large blue lake. The boat, with its nine passengers, sped out over the waters, creating a large bow spray.

Meeting With the Dreamer Chiefs

It was dark as the Old Man idled the boat into the dock at their destination. A man held a lantern high, guiding them into the dock, and Bran tossed him the bowline, which he secured to a dock post.

The man was Susquona, the Old Man's son, and a chief in his own right. Willow and Falcon had been together with Susquona in a Dreamer's Ceremony when they had come here years before. He was a tall handsome man with long black hair. By the lantern's light his dark pupils shone in a face that looked like a mask of polished walnut.

"Hello Willow. Hello Falcon. It's good to see you again," Susquona said as he helped them from the boat, clasping each of their hands in a welcoming grip.

"It's good they have brought each of you," he said to the three couples as they stepped out of the boat. "I'm Susquona, and I'll be with you, along with my parents, the Dreamer Chiefs, during your stay here. We have much to look into together, and your insights will be important in helping to see what needs to be understood at this time."

The group had loaded their gear on the dock and began shouldering their packs and walking when Steve turned and asked where the Old Man was. Everyone turned around and looked back at the boat. In the shadowy light cast by the lantern there was no sign of the Old Man who had brought them there.

"Oh he's probably bringing my mother descriptions of you all so she won't feel left out," smiled Susquona. "Come give me a hand with the chest of fish and the bread Susan sent. We don't want to leave it for the bears and raccoons."

"I don't get it!" cried Steve. "How'd he get past us? Any of you see him go?"

Everyone shook their heads, and then Susquona spoke. "It's okay. The Old Man's a tricky one. Slips by me, too, sometimes. Come on, I'll take you to your cabin where you can get some food and put out your bedrolls. After you've eaten I'll come back with the Old Man and Old Woman, and we'll talk about tomorrow."

The group followed Susquona, casting quizzical looks at one another. Steve came last, peering in the darkness around the boat and then shaking his head. "Damn!" he said as he followed the others.

As the group settled into the large comfortable cabin, each one of them was deep in their own thoughts, reflecting on their impressions of the trip. While blowing up their air mattresses and setting out their bedrolls, there was little conversation. By the light of the oil lamps, their features and movements were bathed in soft light, and the play of shadow gave them a mysterious and timeless look. They could have been a group of humans from anytime or anyplace. They were each feeling this sense of magic and reflecting on it.

Later, when they gathered to make sandwiches and coffee in the rustic kitchen, Eva was the first one to speak. "We are all experienced in the mystery and beauty that comes from being in ceremony and guiding others that have come to be with us, but I feel at this moment as if it is a first time for all of us. I am touched, and feel a sense of timeless beginning."

Eva's statement opened a time of sharing among the little circle of travelers. In turn, each of them spoke of the deep impression the experience was having on them: the flight north from Winnipeg in the old twin-engine monoplane, over the vast forested regions; the silence of their walk to the lake; the meeting with Stan and Susan and the cordiality of their reception; meeting and riding with the Old Man over the deep waters of the lake in silence; arriving on the darkened island, greeted by Susquona; and, lastly, the Old Man's disappearing in the night.

As they spoke of the impact of these events, they became aware of a collective sense of the mystery and import of this time. Something was opening to them, like the parting of clouds at night, revealing a panoply of stars in limitless space.

Willow and Falcon listened carefully to their words of reflection and shared similar thoughts. From years of training and ceremony spent with the group, Willow and Falcon knew their little band well. Deep trust and trained consciousness bound them together, creating a rich and profound sense of family.

It had not always been so. Willow and Falcon remembered marrying the large Scotsman, Bran, and the beautiful and sensitive Katherine years ago on an island off the coast of Scotland. It was a second marriage for each of them, drawn together by a common yearning, but still carrying the tentativeness that came from unfulfilled expectations, misunderstanding, and past disappointments.

CHAPTER SIX—*The Call to the North*

Bran and Katherine were at the closing of their forties, and in the past years they had worked diligently in the Medicine Way on their relationship. They forged a strong and interdependent quality of mutual respect that gave off a warm aura of stability to those around them.

Into the quiet sharing came the poignant long cry of a loon on the lake. This bird of the northlands was considered by the Cree people to carry the medicine of memory. Hearing its sound seemed to draw their thoughts to the past. In the silent kitchen the group appeared to do just that, each of their faces reflecting an introspective stillness, going back in time.

"I feel somehow as if I've been here before," spoke Kurt, breaking the spell-like quiet. "Ever since crossing the depth of that beautiful lake out there, I feel I can almost grasp it in my hands. It took me back to my childhood and sailing across Starnberger See with my father in a small sailboat. I remember him saying 'there is mystery in the deep waters.' Well, I feel we're all in 'it' now," he said, smiling and making quote signs with the first two fingers of each hand for the word "it."

Kurt was a stocky and quick-moving person with a bright smile and eyes that became intense and focused the instant he came to an issue that needed solving. He had learned martial arts in his 20s, while living in Japan and working with a stock trading firm. That was where he met the lithe and sensual Eva. She had been studying painting. They had married upon returning to southern Bavaria and continued their careers. Kurt's probing intellect had drawn him to seek more real and pragmatic solutions to the issues he saw his country and the world facing. After some excursions into vision questing and meditation, Kurt had met Falcon and Willow in Germany and decided to join a medicine training program with them. That was a turning point in Kurt and Eva's lives.

Eva joined Kurt in his medicine work, and after two years they developed a training for German business leaders, which incorporated the medicine teachings and art. Two years ago this energetic couple appeared at Falcon's and Willow's institute and announced they wanted to become part of the team of medicine keepers who were taking the teachings into the world. They were both in their early 40's then, a time often spoken of in the medicine path as the Gateway.

A knock sounded on the cabin door, and Willow went over to open it. Standing on the porch in the dim light were three figures. Susquona stood tall and stately, wearing a bright white tunic, belted at the waist. A red scarf around his head framed his bronzed face and dark braids. Each of his braids carried an eagle feather. Tight jeans and moccasins completed his dress. His presence emanated the chief that he was.

Slightly back and to either side of Susquona were the two Dreamer Chiefs. On the left stood an elderly woman, full in figure with a round, moon-shaped face that had both the beauty of a cloud and the knowing wisdom of the ages. The Old Woman wore a headband of black beads with a pattern of white diamond shapes around her forehead. Her silver hair was plaited down her back. She carried on her left forearm a turquoise colored blanket with a purple and black design. A fringed leather dress flowed from her shoulders to her small moccasin feet.

On the right stood the Old Man, but now his chiseled face was framed by a beaded headdress, with eagle feathers and white fur strips hanging down—the traditional headdress of a male Dreamer Chief. He wore a red and white vertical-striped medicine shirt, fringed buckskin trousers, and beaded moccasins. His brown elegant hands held the traditional medicine pipe, sitting on a large disk of black obsidian.

"We have come to begin ceremony with you," he said. "We bring our blessings and welcome you and all your family and your people."

Chapter Seven
The Kiva Experience

Entering the Kiva

In the center of the island was a high mound-shaped hill covered with tall grass that waved in ripples as the breeze from the lake blew across it. The mound was about 25 feet high and appeared to be approximately 60 feet in diameter, with a tunnel-like opening at the eastern base.

Led by Susquona the following morning, the group walked single file to the tunnel opening, where they stopped. At a signal from Susquona, a Cree man and women entered the tunnel mouth and disappeared into the darkness. In a few moments the muffled sounds of a rhythmic drumming could be heard from inside the earth mound.

One by one, with the Dreamer Chiefs leading, the group entered the dark tunnel and soon stepped into a small vestibule-like space. The walls and curved ceiling were covered with slabs of limestone that were imprinted with myriad textures, fossilized impressions of shells and other sea life. Opposite the tunnel entrance, and set into the limestone wall, was a pair of wooden doors with carved designs of old glyphs, which looked Mayan in character. The floor was covered with black slate, cut in diamond shapes and set flush with one another. In the subdued light coming from the tunnel entrance, the limestone seemed to glow, soft and iridescent.

Susquona reached up and pulled down a series of hides that were fastened to a ledge where the curved ceiling met the tunnel entrance. The vestibule immediately became totally dark and seemed to expand in infinite space. Each one of the group stood in expectant silence. The drumming sound that came from beyond the carved wood doors grew louder, yet had a soft muffled quality that was soothing, like a gentle heart beat.

After a few minutes of stillness, measured by the sounds of the heart drum, the wooden doors opened, revealing a large spherical-shaped arena. Around the arena's perimeter were torches, burning with a golden glow that filled the space and spilled into the small vestibule. Below the landing, where the people stood upon entering, was a series of concentric rings or ledges, in descending steps, like an amphitheater. At the bottom of the spherical space was a black shining flat circle of obsidian, about six feet in diameter. It was surrounded by the lowest tier of the ledges. Overhead the dome rose upward, completing the sphere. All of the surfaces were covered with the textured limestone, similar to the vestibule.

This was a Kiva.

The soft rhythm of the muffled drum beats and the glow of golden light deeply impacted the perception of each of the humans that comprised the group. Each of them was held in a sensory experience that was both arousing and gently encompassing at the same moment.

From across the sphere the two Dreamer Chiefs motioned Willow and Falcon's group to their seats on the tier level with the entrance. When all were seated the Old Man raised his hand and the drumming ceased. In a low voice, yet clearly audible to every person around the sphere, he informed them that this was the Dreamer Chiefs' realm. Here the seekers will immerse themselves and open their understanding about the time of transition prophesized on the Mother Earth.

"We will share with you what has come to us as dreamers that will enable the human people to emerge and flower during this time of transition," the Old Woman Dreamer Chief said. "Two primary understandings of the Medicine Way that you all carry will be opened wider in this ceremony. The first is the illusionary quality of time and space."

"The second understanding that we are called to open with you in this ceremony is the perception of cycles. These cycles permeate the awareness of past, present and future for us humans," spoke the Old Man Dreamer Chief.

The Nature of Reality

"The first of these two understandings—that of our Medicine Way of perceiving the nature of reality—will be opened with you during this first day in the Kiva," continued the Old Woman Dreamer Chief. "Then tomorrow morning, outside the Kiva, after your night's rest, we will speak of the Medicine Way of understanding the cyles of our human journey. These two teachings will prepare you for the next four days, traveling in the memory of the Medicine Singers through the cycles of our human story. We will now begin."

As a very soft resonant beat on the drum made a background of sound, the two Dreamers began chant-like speaking, first one and then the other. As their poetic words flowed, silent figures extinguished the torches one by one, until the Kiva was in total darkness.

The words of their measured chant formed patterns of imagery in the minds of the listening group. The soft drumming sound, the cadence of spoken words, and the darkness all allowed the being state of awareness to become all encompassing. Consciousness was like the still, dark mirror of a deep pond, limitless, boundless, yet alive. Their words became like drops that spread in concentric rings of thought and merged with the Source.

The Dreamer Chiefs spoke of all events as one event, all universes as one song, all beginnings as one moment of creation, where spirit flowed in limitless manifestation, like endless cloud formations, merging, separating, and merging again in ever-forming patterns and shapes.

"Birth and death are one thing," they spoke. "They are but different portals where spirit flows in one deathless circle.

"The densest stone is permeable to the spirit, as is the heart of the tree or the eye of the flying eagle. All 'I's are but one 'I,' seeing itself.

"The Sacred Dream of Life that we humans experience as reality is a gossamer weaving of illusory sensation.

"Time is born of the sensation of space. The subtle organs of receptive perception weave energy to form shape, texture, distance, and movement.

"That which is formed is formless energy arising from the womb of life and yet still a mystery, a unity that is not one and yet not many.

"Our collective human consciousness is now called to pass through boundaries that do not exist; through time, through space, to our source of stillness that is the Being of All Movement.

"These are the messages that stars have sent to us in the darkness of the night sky," completed the Dreamer Chiefs.

As each member of the group was in the experience of ceremonial energy, they let the flow of sounds, words, and sensations in this extraordinary environment flow through them without trying to grasp at straws of significance. Each person took individual responsibility to watch the patterns of thought that arose within them, letting blossom and expand the unique understanding they knew was being evoked. All sense of time had fallen away and the darkness held no boundaries of dimension. It was like being in the heart of the universe.

Willow saw intricate patterns in a spectrum of colors, shifting patterns of delicate arches and spheres imprinted on the darkness of space. These began to form themselves into shapes of intertwined flowers and leaves. Emerging through this foliage was an eye that became the eye of an eagle. And the beats of the eagle's mighty wings carried her consciousness aloft, far above the rounded form of the Mother Earth. There, through the eagle's eyes, she could see the continents surrounded by blue oceans. She, Eagle, sensed the movement of forests, grasses, and both animal and human kind in movement. Her last thought before entering the dream state were the words "must pass through boundaries that do not exist."

In the darkness of the Kiva, the dreaming mind of each of the group had merged into the pool of collective remembrance.

Outside, Grandfather Sun had completed his journey across the sky. One by one the torches were lit again as the members of the group surfaced from the pool of their collective dreaming. Susquona stood up and signaled them to follow him as he left the Kiva.

Outside, standing by the hill mound enclosing the Kiva, the sky was alight with brilliant stars, and the air was filled with the perfumed breath of the surrounding forest. Motioning the group to form around him, Susquona said, "The Old Man and Old Woman have told me to tell you some things. They said we each are to contemplate our experience and to let our understanding emerge from what we have heard and seen in our Kiva time.

"They also said," he continued, "that they see our collective human destiny in this time as like the butterfly, emerging from its cocoon. In numerous places and times in our collective history, they said, thought has risen from the visionary mind of great teachers, thought which is free of space-time limitation. The words and actions of these luminous ones have been like beacons, calling humans to the higher destiny of spirit. Now, in this time of completion of another cycle, the collective mind of humans must manifest the freedom to move beneath the surface of the illusory sense of time and space to Spirit's home, while still moving in this world of beauty."

With the completion of Susquona's sharing of the words of the Old Ones, the seekers moved off to contemplate and rest. They were told to return to the Kiva at dawn.

The Cycles of Human Growth

The next morning the group seated themselves on benches made from split tree trunks. They were grouped around the Dreamer Chiefs, who sat cross-legged on the earth in front of them. Behind the group the Kiva hill mound was silhouetted against the morning sky. The rising sun was shooting long shafts of light into the blue sky through a cluster of white cumulus clouds at the horizon. Susquona had brought a large thermos of coffee and some mugs.

"You all are rested for this day?" the Old Woman queried.

Everyone nodded affirmatively, their faces open, their eyes bright.

"This delicious coffee is helping us get ready," said Bran, laughing. "After the journey yesterday, I'm ready to voyage onward with delight."

Sitting in a circle, they began their stringing of the beads, each person sharing their sense of anticipation as the old chiefs listened. After a few minutes, using a beaded staff, the Old Man began to draw a large circle, spiraling inward, in the sand in front of him. The shadow cast by the early sun's rays brought the perfect curve of the spiral into sharp relief. The Old Man sat, looking down at the design as if he were seeing something moving along the sculpture's ever-widening track.

Finally he raised his face and looked at each one with his piercing dark eyes. "You have been called to be here to understand some awareness the people need in this time," he said. "We have seen, the Old Woman and I, that you and others like you are to carry a message to the people, the humans of this earth."

"What we know, what we have been given to know, with your coming here," spoke the Old Woman slowly as she gestured toward the sky, "is that the message that must be brought to the people is related to the deeper remembrance and understanding of the cycles of our human journey song."

Everyone in the group was leaning forward, alert like wolves sensing their quarry. "What we experienced yesterday in the Kiva," said Willow, pointing to the mound entrance, "was the freedom of our imagination to cross the boundaries of time and space and directly experience those cycles." Willow breathed deeply, narrowing her eyes. "This leads us to the deeper understanding you speak of!" she emphasized.

"Yes, Willow, that is what we have been told," said the Old Man as he lit his pipe. "Medicine Singers, who keep the stories of the people's journeys alive, are able to do so because they can cross barriers of time and space in their images. Thus, they directly experience what it was like to be in those events. This is a power we humans have, but most are not aware of it and do not use it as a disciplined capability."

The Old Woman made a hoop with her arms, the tips of her fingers touching. "Each of us human spirits is wrapped in this body, a body that is a temple of the universe and of the Mother Earth herself," she said smiling. "Our spirit inhabits this temple for a time, as medicine people know, like wearing an overcoat. While living in this temple we dream our dreams fed by information from our body temple, which itself is made of the energy of the universe."

The Old Woman paused, looking at each of them, her hands now folded in her lap. "We know that you understand this because of who you are and what you are doing in this life. But we all know," she continued, "that the young are no longer taught these things. They do not know that they are spirits residing in a temple of remembrance. Most of them have been given little or no guidance or understanding of this knowledge. And so generations grow up in ignorance of how to listen to the information this body temple gives them. Thus, they reside with a wealth of information, which they do not understand or even recognize. Instead, they grow up thinking all information comes from outside of them. They become driven and react in confusion. They look for someone to lead them who appears to have power or 'knows' and can provide for them. In this way they create a source for their own dependency."

Each of the individuals in the group thought of their own learning and growing-up process, where all instruction seemed to point outward to what was needed to be successful, or admired, or to feel loved or appreciated. And each felt a deep appreciation for the teaching and training they had been drawn to in their hungry search for meaning. They had learned and remembered in a different way.

"A long evolution of our human consciousness has been needed to uncover the realization of our human role in this sacred Dream of Life," spoke the Old Man as he stood up. "Many of the tribal cultures of earth peoples all over the world have come to this same understanding of the mystery of our human consciousness and the part it plays in the threads of Mother Earth's life."

Lighting his pipe again, and slowly pacing in front of the group, he continued. "They taught their children this accumulated understanding over generations and taught them how to play their unique part in this collective dream. Our ancestors, these earth people, were part of a long cycle of the evolution of this collective human consciousness. This time may be seen as the 'innocent stage' of the collective human family's development. If we can see our human journey as a growing organism of intelligence, we can imagine this long cycle as the age of childhood, with its bright and trusting development, just as it is in the individual healthy human."

The Old Man stopped and looked into the faces of each of the listeners. "Can you imagine this with us?" he asked, holding his hand out to the Old Woman. She reached out, took his hand, and gracefully rose to her feet.

"Of course you can!" The Old Woman said with a big smile. "This day is still young, with Grandfather Sun still rising above the clouds in the east. You have all come a long way on your journeys to be here for this time of introspection and inquiry. Let us continue."

Indeed, each of the group was excited with the revealing play of imagery. They were also surprised by how small an arc the sun had traversed since they had begun. They felt as if they had traveled long and far, imagining the time of the human organism's early growth as the tribal earth cultures.

As the Old Woman continued, she called to mind that the healthy human child was endowed with a brilliance of illumination because of its ability to visualize and imagine. She also pointed out that such a child was immensely inventive and increasingly skillful as its capacity for innovation and creativity developed. Its capacity continued to develop as it overcame obstacles and barriers.

"There is tremendous resilience in such a child, as it expands its experience and adventures deeper into the realm of curiosity and understanding," she added.

"Let us now imagine this whole long journey of development and apply it to all humans, as one organism of collective humanity. For a long cycle of many thousands of years this organism has been growing through this magical experience, emerging and developing itself in what we might describe as its childhood."

The Old Man spoke again. "If we hold this way of seeing, we can be aware that many times of expansion and bright moments of brilliance occurred again and again during the organism's development. We can also see times of contraction and assimilation, as well as periods of confusion, fright, and reaction—just like the evolution of the individual human child."

Both the old Dreamer Chiefs went on to elaborate this image of the organism called "humanity" in its increasing growth and expansion. It experiences an increasingly complex state of consciousness until its size and diversity bring it to an age that the old couple referred to as an "age of adolescence."

"This time of adolescence may have begun some ten thousands years ago," said the Old Woman. "We can imagine this collective humanity coming into an age where changing times and energies impacted it, forcing it to cope with larger and more demanding needs.

"This began a period called civilization, when experimentation in organization and the accumulation of material well-being dominated the organism's focus," continued the Old Woman. "During this period more and more of the practices and natural wisdom of the earlier age were cast aside as not being adequate to meet the needs that the governing structures deemed necessary."

During this period, in what the Old Man and Old Woman called humanity's adolescence, the seekers saw a great shift in an increasing attention to the outer aspects of life. There was less and less awareness of the inner life and the world of the spirit. The direct relationship with the Life Mystery was lost.

"Cultures grew which were increasingly focused on gathering and manipulating the richness of Mother Earth, rather than caring for and loving Her beautiful and delicate diversity," the Old Man pointed out. "A whole new sense of power, based on force and conforming behavior, began to dominate the human consciousness. It was characterized by heavy judgment, discrimination, and extinction of that which deviated."

"Vast wars and exploitative behavior were characteristic of this adolescence," spoke the Old Woman. "At the same time many beautiful items were created, and wondrous discovery was fostered by this accelerated and expanding growth. War and conquest often gave birth to advances in the human organism's quest for greater control over its environment. However, the cost was immense. Perhaps the loss of the sense of the sacredness of life was the greatest cost."

Continuing, the Old Man said, "Much other valuable wisdom of the early journey song of humanity was discarded or destroyed also. Those who called themselves philosophers and priests took an increasing role in dictating how the people should think and act. Generations of the human tide surrendered and never knew the ways of the early cultures of earth people, who fostered the development of the self as a sacred spirit flower of the Life Mystery."

"Very important in this shift of consciousness from the inner to the outer forms of human consciousness was the change in the balance of roles of women and men," the Old Woman said. "In the period of the organism's adolescence, the role and function of men for the most part dominated the role of women in determining the meaning and expression of the organism's cultures and values. Before this, during the early times of the earth people, there was a balance in these functions."

"In conclusion," the Old Man said, "bright gems in our human journey continued to exist during this time. Shards of beauty and brilliance continued to call to the heart of humanity to awake to its true destiny, to know the spirit flowering of the people's hearts all over the Mother Earth."

"We have spoken many words with this rising of the Grandfather Sun," said the Old Woman. "They have been breathed to you in the morning air, calling you forward in the mind and memory of the Medicine Singer."

The Four-Day Medicine Singer Journey

"We will soon enter the Kiva, where you will experience this long cycle of humanity directly into your consciousness. This is the old way of the Medicine Singers, using the power of imagination," said the Old Man.

"We are here to learn something important for all our people in this transition time," said the Old Woman as she looked up into the blue sky of the Mother Earth's aural atmosphere. "These next days we will participate in a special kind of fast as we go on this journey song of remembrance of our human family."

The old couple then told the seekers that they would travel this last epoch of 52,000 years of the human journey song in much the same way as each of them had done in their individual journey song ceremonies during their training. They explained that they would all search for wisdom gems in this story of the people's growth from the childhood era to the adolescent era, looking for clues and patterns that might guide humanity toward a passage into a new era—the beginning of adulthood consciousness and spiritual responsibility.

The first day in the Kiva, they were informed, would be a passing through the memories of 46,000 cycles of the earth around the sun. The second day they would pass through 5,000 cycles. The last two days, as Medicine Singers in the Kiva meditation, they would be passing through the last 1000 years, including the last 100 years of the human journey.

"As this great cycle of 52,000 years comes to completion, the last hundred years will hold important signs for the future of humanity, as there is great acceleration in the completion of such a vast cycle," explained the Old Man, using his staff to point to the center of the sand spiral.

"Now we will prepare ourselves to enter the Kiva," said the Old Woman. She began singing a guttural chant and shaking a deer-hoof rattle as she walked slowly toward the entrance of the Kiva. The old man walked behind her, and the seekers followed. When each of the group entered the Kiva, with its high domed ceiling and the descending rings of stepped ledges, they were impacted with the strong fragrance of sweetgrass perfuming the air.

A change of energy and a vibration was felt as they looked about. The seating ledges were covered with brightly colored medicine blankets folded over thick mattresses. The beautiful designs on the blankets stood out sharply against the creamy limestone interior. These rings of designs drew their eyes down, step by step, to the obsidian disk at the bottom of the spherical space. Around the rim of the jet black disk was a ring of burning candles. The circular disk now seemed like a dark round window into a space far below them.

Most startling to the group was a large polished gray ball that now appeared suspended above the middle of the topmost ring of seats, at the entrance level where the group now stood. Closer inspection showed the ball to be held by a thin white wire connected to the center of the dome. Its mass, floating there, was impressive to the senses. The ball seemed to be several feet in diameter, but the sense of distance in the space was elusive.

"That stone sphere," said the Old Man, "was sent to us from Costa Rica. There are hundreds of them in the jungles there of different sizes, all of this same perfectly spherical shape. No one knows how our ancestors shaped them or why, but we are given to understand that they were for a practice of contemplation."

You will see," the Old Woman added, as she pointed each of the seekers to one of the top-level mattresses. "Sit and be comfortable now, and start breathing slowly with the rhythm of the drum. We will start our journey song as Medicine Singers in the great cycle 52,000 years ago."

The measured, deep, slow, steady beat of a large drum moved through the space, like a strong heart beat. Its vibration filled the bodies and consciousness of the people

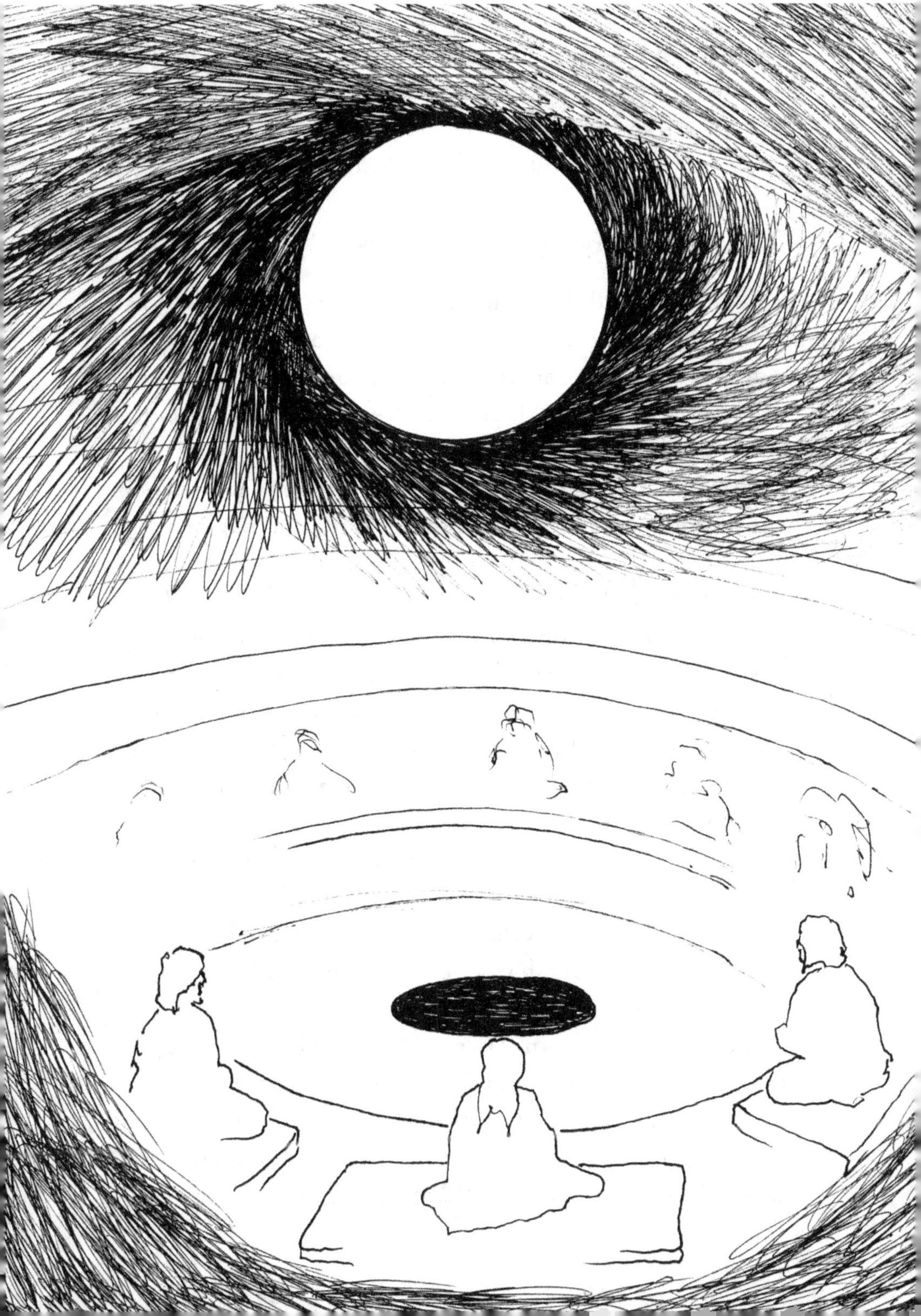

Chapter Seven—*The Kiva Experience*

as they sank into the mind of the Medicine Singer experiencing past memory. One by one the torches were extinguished until the floating globe was illuminated only by the soft flickering light of the candle ring far below. The black mirror seemed to open out into the universe.

The First Day—46,000 Years

The darkened dome appeared to disappear. The great stone orb floated in space, washed in golden moving tides from the flickering candles far below. As the seekers looked downward from their seats, the black circular space of the obsidian mirror seemed to open.

Deeper and deeper, the orb drew the consciousness of those present to itself. Its color shifted to a pale blue, then green, then white, and then patterns of red and ocher appeared against the blue. It became alive and drew the sensate mind into itself. Textures and the colors of land masses were revealed, surrounded with blue oceans and turning patterns of white cloud formations. The beautiful earth planet filled more and more of the mind's eye as it held the seekers' awareness, and they gazed in fascination.

Home. Long, long ago. A touching down in lush forested foliage. Silence at first, then a soft brushing of the skin followed by a thrumming flutter and graze of wings. Senses keen, sharpened, taut and ready. Sight, sound, smell, taste and touch—alive.

This was the dominant consciousness impressed upon the Medicine Singer awareness. What moved in shape and form was life, both inner and outer, no separation.

A tug on the consciousness of the Medicine-Singer mind drew attention to a widening arc of awareness and remembrance of the human journey of experience in this vast expanse of time. A flowing, shifting pattern of imagery moved the vision to an eagle's view, across forest and plain, across mountains and valleys and the vast expanse of oceans. Again it moved over dense jungle and river deltas, over shifting images of textured land mass. Then movement was seen; great herds of animals and separate mammoth beasts and stalking hunters, some great catlike beings, others armed with weapons and walking on two legs. The latter were humans, part of the life manifestation of this Mother Planet. Here, with the advent of the humans, begins the focus of the Medicine Singer quest of remembrance.

In the constantly shifting patterns of imagery these beings were seen in small family-like clusters, sometimes hunkering close together in cave or glen, sometimes filing along paths made by animals, or spread wide on beaches or plains, stooping to gather from the earth then and moving again, ever alert and moving in concert, like schools of fish or flocks of birds. They shared a bond of consciousness with one another. They were a unit, a being of sensate intelligence with one focus, to survive and to continue.

Merging closer in this vision of remembrance, the group's Medicine Singer consciousness deeply sensed these widely-scattered groups of humanity, as they lived their lives in the richness and fecundity of the Mother Earth. As the waves of generations passed before them, the Medicine Singers felt the times of plenty and the times of scarcity and danger with these beings. They saw and felt the impact of the changes in the Mother Earth's form as ice and snow drove the small bands to new lands. Celestial beings seemed to fall across the night skies and impressed the consciousness of these tight little bands, bringing sounds of awe from their throats.

As wave after wave of generations passed in their vision, spreading and leaving the mark of their presence on the sands of time, the Medicine Singers saw and felt the consciousness of this two-legged species grow in skill, cleverness and form. They adapted and grew. Female and male, young and old wove increasingly complex patterns of providing for life's needs. Delicate rituals and practices were enacted as the part of life the Medicine Singers were experiencing in their memory. The small bands grew larger and spread throughout ever-expanding areas of the earth.

Forms of teaching, play, and ceremonies occupied more and more of this conscious entity called humanity, as successive hundreds of generational cycles passed in image across the remembrance mind of the Medicine Singers. A long period of relative stability gradually settled among these humans.

A period of many thousand cycles passed, where territories were determined and the larger bands moved slowly in patterns of the seasons within familiar areas, which they claimed. The consciousness of the people deepened in this epoch, and the Medicine Singers felt the increasing subtlety and sophistication of the minds of the people, as their thoughts were shaped by the delicate fabric of life.

They felt the thoughts of the people as they lived their lives in relationship with the plants and animals and the life around them. The Medicine Singers heard the people's minds—thoughts of connection and relationship with the land and all the living things that were part of Mother Earth. As the people hunted, gathered, ate, made love, gave birth, encountered death, and explored the meaning that the stars sent them, the Medicine Singers melded with their consciousness. The people's hopes and dreams, their joys and sorrows were known in the hearts of the Medicine Singers. They remembered the people's stories because they were their stories too.

The journey of this long cycle of human consciousness, 46,000 cycles, was coming to completion in the visionary mind of the Medicine Singers. Countless images had passed before their awareness, imprinting deeply upon their labyrinths of memory. Light began to fill the Kiva space as each of them drew gradually back from the depth of the ocean of recalled experience. They each felt they had lived this long cycle.

In their altered state, thought images continued to dance, and they recalled the final stages of the journey from which they had just returned. Numberless clusters of people's fires burned on every continent of the Mother Earth, and here and there upon Her breast they had also seen great amassing of people's presence. These great congregations were markedly different from the simple villages that dotted the continents. These swarming metropolises had great buildings and avenues lined with temples and plazas for trade and societal activity. In this phenomenon the seekers had seen the beginnings of a great change in the journey song of humanity's consciousness.

Rising and stretching back into their present body-minds, each of the group filed out of the Kiva entrance into the night, brilliant with stars. A soft breeze blew off the lake, sighing through the pine trees and caressing each one with a blessing of return. After a silent walkabout the seekers returned to sleep in the darkened Kiva.

The Second Day—5,000 Years

Beginning the second day of the Kiva Ceremony, the Medicine Singers awakened from sleep. That's how they thought of themselves now, as the Medicine Singers. The sound of the great drum resonated a deep booming call as they rose from their beds. The step tier they now occupied was several levels down from the entry level where they had begun yesterday. Fresh torches had been lit.

Large cups of fresh water and bowls of blueberries were lifted from the tray by the Old Woman and passed to each seeker. Each of the members of the group ate the simple repast in silence. They noticed that the stone sphere was above their eye level now and the obsidian mirror below them was closer and seemed larger.

They knew that today they would be drawn deeply into the cycle of the most recent 5,000 years of the human journey. This would bring them closer to the prophesied end of the great 52,000-year passage. They recalled that they had seen the beginning evidence of a great shift in several places on the Mother Earth. In these places was seen an increasing amassing of people in great metropolises surrounded by deforested and cultivated lands. The Medicine Singers had felt strongly the shift in the collective consciousness of humanity as awareness of this change spread.

Now, as the torches were extinguished, they were once again drawn into the vision of the Mother Earth's turning. They experienced the flow of images generated by the wave-like passage of more than 200 generations of humans.

At first remembrance of the onset of this change, they still felt strongly the stable, long-established patterns of the Earth people's consciousness across the lands. The ways of balance and harmony with life continued as a strong pulse of energy consciousness around the many villages and tribal lands of humanity. Then, with each passing generational wave, the Medicine Singers saw and felt the spread of a new form of consciousness as it enveloped more and more of humanity's attention away from its old way of living with nature.

Across large areas of the Mother Earth's lands there began to spread systems of social culture devoted to agriculture and storage that provided for the needs of larger and larger population centers. Old hunting and gathering practices and the tribal life systems, which allowed the migratory life to hold together and flourish, were supplanted in these areas of dense human population.

Collective tribal government was supplanted by hierarchical forms of authority. Ownership of land and its resources became the practice, and enforcement of social customs was carried out by echelons of troops and administrators at the directive of the ruling select.

A significant element of this change deeply affected the manifestation of the spiritual life of humanity. With the growth of hierarchical forms of control and governance, dominated by men, the role of women in the previous tribal matrilineage culture was eliminated. With this shift began a significant spiritual transition, which emphasized and worshiped a male deity. There began a separation from the presence in nature of the divine that honors both the feminine mother and the masculine father. This shift fostered a change in attitude toward the Mother Earth. Mother Earth was no longer seen as a living being to be listened to, honored, and respected.

The Third Day—1000 Years

Once again the Medicine Singers had slept in the Kiva, on their ledges. Now, on this third day of the Dreamer Chiefs' Ceremony, the Medicine Singers sat in meditation on one of the lower ledges close to the black mirror and its ring of candles. Immersed far beneath the surface in their journey of time travel, the thoughts of the Medicine Singers flowed unbroken into the last millennia of humanity's journey, in what the Dreamer Chiefs had called its "age of adolescence."

They gazed upward with barely opened eyes at the ever-turning vision of the Mother Earth as images formed of the people's journey in the last fifty generations, or 1000 years. There arose ages of human activity marked by brilliant epochs of creative expression in a turmoil of city-state struggles, as each vied for control. Movements over land and water by intrepid small bands of explorers connected people and cultures through conquest and subjugation, claiming and absorbing, trading and marauding, a ceaseless ebb and flow of movement, like the tide pools at the ocean's restless shore.

What compass of thought guides these spreading sheets of the generations, shimmering wavelets on the shores of life? All around the lands of Mother Earth Her human children have been drawn into a succession of litanies of identity called religion. Each of these religions claimed the righteous and true understanding of the meaning of life, having been given by the teachings and enlightenment of great spiritual leaders. Those who followed these enlightened visionaries had translated their gifted insights into codified doctrines. In time, these doctrines were imposed by those holding religious authority and those who sought power and control, upon the hearts and minds of the people.

Deification was endowed upon the heads of lineages, who, with pomp, held scepters of authority and directed the pursuit of material acquisition from thrones of hierarchical rank and privilege. Self knowledge and inquiry had been replaced by rote catechisms in the garden of childhood's growth. The Mother Earth had become an object to be explored and exploited. She was assigned an image as a place of trial and tribulation, which the spirit must endure before going to a heavenly destiny. Those humans still holding Her as a source of identity and respect, as the Mother Womb of the Life Mystery, were hunted, persecuted and branded as unworthy of human dignity. Many were put to death.

In this final epoch of humanity's adolescence, concepts of reality and time that reduced our Mother Planet to mere lifeless matter were impressed on the consciousness of the people. Her children became subjects to be controlled and exploited.

Flowing like a great river, the images and experience of humanity's journey lit the memory mind of the Medicine Singers, where light reflected from the water's rippling surface. The shuttle of the loom of time wove more images in the Medicine Singers' vision.

Great edifices of religious and secular power arose, which created a sense of awe and submissive acceptance in the hearts of the people. Crusading travelers returned carrying old and esoteric knowledge from far lands, awakening the seeds of curiosity. Words and ideas flowed more quickly onto printed pages, and these sparked bright energies in inquisitive minds.

The Medicine Singers see the gradual growth of national identities, which built the people into a tighter world of relationship. Shining empires spread their claims around the earth, harvesting the fruits of many lands to increase their treasury's wealth, often decimating the old earth cultures in their wake.

In time, the burgeoning of new thought and ideas gave rise to ingenious play, invention, and more experimentation. This activity birthed an industrial cornucopia which fed and nourished some of the children, but depleted and enslaved many others. One result of this stimulus of human renaissance was an awakening in the hearts and minds of many peoples of the earth. They dreamed of freedom and human dignity and brought forth experiments in new forms of governance.

The Medicine Singers see that across the lands great promise and great expectations flourished as the dawn of the second millennium's last century approached. However, they are also aware that there are many millions of the human family whose voices and needs are unheard and uncared for.

With these visions in their minds, the third day ends, and the Medicine Singers lie down to rest and sleep.

The Fourth Day—100 Years

Beginning their last day in the Kiva Ceremony, the Medicine Singers awaken early. They immediately experience a collective vision that has a powerful impact on them.

Across the vast dome of darkness, the jagged forks of lightening pierce and pierce again the vision with brilliant shards of light. Storm clouds cover the star-filled night and rolling waves of thunder fill the sky.

Thousands of human babies, girls and boys, are seen to emerge from the mother's womb this night. They are the most recent fragile line of human life to arrive on the shores of time. This is the beginning of the generations of humanity born into the twentieth century and the year is numbered 1900, by the prevailing calendars of reckoning.

Quietly, the Medicine Singers move to the lowest ledge of the Kiva and seat themselves around a circle of candles, which surrounds the black obsidian mirror. The light from the candles seems to shimmer off the surface of the mirror, and each of the group experiences its beckoning aliveness. Now, their gaze turns upward, toward the sphere above them, glowing in the darkness. Already they have traveled in the mind to the Mother Earth's presence in this last cycle they are called to remember in this Kiva time.

The collective image they have just experienced as they entered the Twentieth Century—the birth of so many of the human children—has deeply touched them. They see that these babes and the millions that follow them will be the people who experience this most recent journey of humanity. They and their children and their children's children will be touched and shaped by this closing cycle of humanity's adolescence. This will be an evolutionary call of awakening, the beginning of the era of the human organism maturing into a vast new potential. These waves of people will move into a new age and cycle, humanity's adulthood.

What elements will shape this completing cycle of humanity's collective consciousness as it approaches this rite of passage into a new world? This question was held in the mind of the Medicine Singers as they continued their journey.

Images of homes, dwellings, and work places of the people everywhere on the Mother Earth passed before their eyes. Some were fashioned and adorned with the latest of civilization's construction materials. Some were humble and tidy, but most were rude shelters with a scarcity of ornamentation.

In the large metropolitan areas, people young and old spent long days in factories and workhouses, in offices and shops, in mines and sites of fabrication. In endless villages and rural spaces, the greatest numbers of the people still worked upon the land from dawn to dusk. At night they found their way to their separate homes, to eat, to talk, to dream and scheme, to make love, to care for the young, and to sleep.

What bound these human spirits to their sense of identity other than the necessary call to sustain their livelihood? The Medicine Singers saw that within each heart and mind still existed the dreams and hopes that have called humanity along its journey. But how often and how widely were these yearnings shared and encouraged to flower?

In the halls within chambers of government, in palaces and in offices of power, schemes were hatched and dreams told that would soon touch the people's lives, as they had done for ages past. So also there was prolific scheming and dreaming in laboratories, universities and workshops, where many gifted minds were bringing forth creations that would profoundly alter the web of connectedness of the people's lives.

The Medicine Singers saw flashing by, in this early period of the century, the products of inventive genius that were binding the human community into a consciousness of proximity and interrelatedness—electric lights, the wireless, the car, the airplane, and the radio. These, and many more inventions, sent shocks of energy and movement into the collective consciousness of humans, changing patterns of thought, communication, and behavior. Wonder and amazement, combined with expansive concepts of manifest destiny, overrode any reluctance of the people to engage and play with this proliferation of human ingenuity. This fascination and impact drew the focus and attention of the human consciousness deeper into the absorption of material possession, and the process of scientific thought gave rise to new values and priorities.

In the last throes of empire consciousness, the storm clouds gathered. Large vessels of opulent pleasure voyaged forth to sink beneath the waves. They were replaced with vessels of destruction that loosed upon the consciousness a hell of human destruction. The people's sons from every land were called upon to fertilize the fields beneath colored banners of righteous authority granted by accommodating deities.

Two generations participated in great rituals of this madness of war in the first half of the last 100 years, and the collective consciousness of the people began to stir in revulsion and revolt. Voices were raised that called for other forms of governance and participation.

Questions of equality and rights fermented, as a tightened sense of relationship of diverse cultures and social practice emerged—suffrage of right to vote, submission of peoples to foreign rule, disempowerment through discriminations of race. All these were challenged and caused turbulence in the social fabric of all nations of people around the Mother Earth.

In the later part of the 20th century, media communications, including cinema, television, video, and computer technology, permeated the awareness of the people and penetrated every community with its images and messages. Conflicts, wars, depredations, and protests became part of the people's diet of information. Dreams also were broadcast, and individuals like Ghandi, Nelson Mandela, and Martin Luther King Jr. gave voice to the people's hearts.

Walls of separation were breaking down in this contracting world of connectedness. At the same time an increasing outpouring of technological wizardry brought speed and unequal distribution of abundance and rapid fluctuation of pressures to outworn systems of management and governance. No coherent governing principles that held the needs of all the people in a balanced council of considerations existed.

At the close of this last century of the millennium, the Medicine Singers see the growing awareness among the people of the great potential of the human family. They also see that this awareness of human capacity is hampered by increased pressure and demands fostered by vast conglomerates of corporate power. These shift rapidly to accommodate changing world markets and economic conditions.

Thrust upon the governments of the nations were voluminous reports of the conditions around the Mother Earth, of her atmosphere, her waters, lands and children, plants, animals, and human. Despite their accords, these governments seemed to lack the collective will and power to affect needed change in how the human family would live in harmonious relationship with each other and the Mother Earth. However, the Medicine Singers could see that more and more clusters of the people were sharing their concerns and sending out messages to others of like mind.

As they ended their Kiva time, looking at the dawning years of a new millennium, the Medicine Singers are aware of the existence of conflict in many places on Mother Earth. They also see the dedication of many people who want to bring peace and harmony. The power of hope among these groups fuels their determination to find the wisdom that will lead humanity toward a new era of health and wholeness.

As the fourth day ended, the Medicine Singers lay down to sleep.

Chapter Eight
The Realization

The Dreamer Chiefs' Words of Guidance

Early the next morning the band of seekers was called to wakefulness, and the torches were lit once again in the Kiva. Using hand signals the Old Woman instructed them to leave the Kiva in silence. As they emerged from the Kiva each was touched by the beauty of the early dawn sky where Namahiah, Grandmother Moon, still shown down on them.

Susquona led the group along a trail to a fire ring at the shore of the lake. As they sat around the fire, sipping their morning tea and eating blueberries, Susquona advised them that the Dreamer Chiefs wished to speak to them of the next step in their ceremony.

The Old Man Dreamer Chief stood and pointed at the large motorboat beached on the shoreline. "You will load your gear in the boat when you finish your breakfast. Today you will travel to an island in the center of the lake. This island is an old sacred site that has been used for a long time by ones who have come to dream."

"You will rest and reflect there," continued the Old Woman Dreamer Chief. "You will reflect on what you have experienced in the Kiva and the signs you see happening in the world in which you currently travel and teach. In two days time, the Old Man and I will join you and hear your words. Then, we will look together for what will further be revealed."

"Good Medicine to you," said the Old Man. Then the old couple turned and walked into the hushed and waiting forest.

To the Island of the Dreamers

Willow and Falcon sat up front in the boat, with Bran and Katherine in the center. The others sat on their gear on either side, with Susquona at the helm. Lively exchanges filled the air as they began the three-hour journey to the island, but after a while each one settled into a companionable silence. As they traveled further and further towards the center of the lake, they each seemed to go deeper and deeper into their own reflections.

They had spent four deeply transforming days with the Dreamer Chiefs and now had two days to rest, reflect and assimilate all they had experienced. The steady sound of the motor seemed to blend with the slapping of the water against the bow of the boat, lulling them into a wonderful reverie. In the center of the lake the azure water appeared bottomless and the land and trees far distant.

Cumulus clouds overhead, occasionally punctuated by flocks of geese, protected them from the steady rays of the sun. In their own way, each prepared for the next part of the journey, knowing it would take them down unexpected pathways.

What they first saw as distant shore now revealed itself as several small islands. Passing them, one by one, the visitors felt a growing sense of anticipation. On they went, with Susquona holding the same deeply focused attention. Out beyond them was one remaining island, small and beautiful. Filled with evergreens and thick stands of birch trees, the Island of the Dreamers lay just ahead. It appeared to be about a mile long and a quarter-mile wide.

Arriving on shore, Susquona smiled and announced, "Okay, everyone, we made it. This is your home for the next couple of days. Let's get you unloaded. I think I can find the old ceremonial site used in ancient times. I was here once with my grandfather when I was a boy. We haven't used this island for many years. It feels good to be here. Welcome to you all."

They jumped out and helped pull the boat onto the shore. Spirits were high as they made fast work of unloading their gear. They each had a backpack, tent with sleeping bag, and a few clothes. Susquona tied off the boat and grabbed the ax and a small bag of supplies.

"Follow me," he said. "There is a place to set up your tents and make a fire. You're on light rations now, but that's good for what lies ahead."

Falcon, right behind Susquona, made a quick check, seeing that everyone was ready. As he walked through the closely growing stands of birch, he gave thought to the last words of Susquona. Not knowing specifically what he meant, he'd had enough experience to take his words seriously and to stay awake.

It didn't take long for them to find the clearing and set up their tents. They all helped gather wood and set up a make-shift wood rack. Susquona said the Old Man and Woman would be coming to meet them in two days time and that they were beginning an ancient purification ritual.

No one asked the purpose of the ritual, but they knew they also needed to make their own preparations. As Susquona was leaving he made it clear they needed to keep their fire going day and night, until the Dreamer Chiefs came to join them.

Reflections

That night, around the fire, they spoke of their impressions of the Kiva ceremony and what they saw would be needed in the two days. Willow began.

"I feel it is no accident that we are here on this island. In my dream in Mexico I was told to find a tree with seeds in the shape of a heart, and just two days ago another dream came where I was on an island like this with the Chiefs of the Nations. I was in a special Dreaming Ceremony with the women chiefs, as they traveled through time. I heard them and saw what they saw as they read the shields of humanity. Now I am much more clear about the significance of the heart seeds. They are a symbol for the dreams and yearnings that are in the hearts of all humans, and now is the time when those seeds need to open. I wonder if this is the same island, even the same place, where the chiefs of ancient times came and where they dreamed forward about the time we live in?"

"I don't know, but I agree with your feeling that this is the opening time," spoke Falcon. "Knowing that, and taking in all that we heard from the Dreamer Chiefs and our Kiva experience, I see how important our two days together will be. We are living in times of turbulence, and it is essential we not lose sight of what is emerging now. The image I have is of a rough sea, with high winds and high waves, but there are islands. Call them islands of awareness. They are like a point of calm, which provides a subtle stability in all the pain and chaos."

"Yes, that is a good image," said Steve. "We need to focus our attention on those islands. They may be like the early signs of the shift of consciousness we have all been praying for."

"These thoughts are a good ground," spoke Eva, "but what are we really looking for? Let's move beyond metaphor and talk reality."

Bran laughed and said, "Sounds just like you, Eva, grounded and real. I'm with you. Let's talk specifics. How about a particular question, like 'What are the shifts in attitude that we can identify?' Attitude reflects what people are thinking, and thought affects consciousness."

"Great," said Eva. "What time frame are we looking at? Is it right now or a longer period?"

Kurt broke in. "Excellent question. My read is that the shift in consciousness has started, and we need to look at the signs of this shift since the new millennium."

"And," spoke Diane, "we don't need to figure everything out tonight. I think, as well, that we need to focus on making this time a ceremony. We all have a sense of the importance of this time and that we are preparing for some next steps, even though we don't clearly know what is ahead. Speaking for myself, I don't want to get caught in too much thinking and analyzing. I propose we stop now and each make silent prayers of intention before we go to our dreams."

"Thank you Diane," said Willow. "I also feel the need to connect more deeply with the land and the spirits here.

This is a good time to shift gears. Who would like to be fire keeper for the next two hours?"

"I'll take the first shift," Falcon volunteered, "and suggest we simply institute a rotation and continue it for these two days. Steve, how about you make up a roster and we'll follow it."

"Glad to," said Steve. "Is that okay with everyone?"

They all spoke their agreement and began their prayer offerings at the fire. A couple of them walked to the water, and each looked deeply into their own intention, asking the spirits to guide them in their explorations.

The First Day of Ceremony

As the sun rose the next morning, the forest seemed to come alive with small birds and other life. They relished the sounds of water lapping on the shore of the nearby lake and the piercing call of the loon, giving an early-morning greeting.

Willow took a walk to see the island and was touched again by the beauty and serenity she felt. She felt other things as well. There was a growing sense of power, like the whole island knew what was happening. She wished she knew what was happening. An incredible journey was unfolding, and she knew all she could do was trust herself to stay open and awake to the spirits that were guiding them.

Returning and looking for Falcon, Willow saw everyone was up and the fire was going strong. The autumn air was brisk, adding a special energy to the shimmering morning. As was their custom, Willow and Falcon put their heads together as they looked at the flow for the day. They agreed that time for morning practice was the first element needed. A light breakfast of tea and jerky would follow. Falcon asked Bran and Katherine to gather everyone for a check-in time.

Since the group had been together in many ceremonies over the years, no one needed to lead anyone else. They all knew what was needed. When they gathered, different members made suggestions at different times. All were considered an equal part of the whole and held their own authority. They each shared decision-making power in the circle, and the way they operated was by agreement.

Quickly they decided they would take an hour, individually, for the first part of their morning practice and then gather at the fire for their community practice. Katherine suggested that during the first hour each find an item from the land to create beauty in the area around the fire, and bring it back. Bran, Steve, and Eva offered to make a small medicine wheel around the fire, and Falcon and Willow offered to share some thoughts about the flow of their ceremony time.

After greeting the spirits and the land during their individual time, the group gathered at the fire and called in the energies of the Sacred Twenty Count. They danced a healing prayer for all life on the planet. Each of them came through a kind of doorway during this time, realizing the deep nature of what they were about to do.

Next, the group chose to go on a walk-about, to contemplate how they saw the turbulence in the world. Later they would together open up what attitudes were beginning to shift and determine what seemed to be emerging.

As they gathered around the sacred fire anyone watching would have wondered who they were. They moved together in a harmony that seemed ancient. Moving deeper into the ceremony, they sat as chiefs looking through wisdom eyes at the present condition of their world.

Silently they came to a deep connection with Chemah, the Sacred Fire. Willow placed sacred prayers into the medicine pipe, while Falcon chanted and worked with the rattle. As the chanting continued each one sent their prayers through the pipe, to the ancestors, asking for guidance in the ceremony time.

Dragonflies danced around them while they sent their thoughts to the Source of All That Is. At the completion of the pipe ceremony two lizards came to the edge of the fire. They both appeared to be doing pushups on the warm stones. Eva and Katherine looked up at the same time, catching each other's eyes with a brief smile and a twinkle of amusement. They knew the lizard carried the dreaming medicine and were thankful for the visit. It was time to begin.

Falcon was the first to speak. "I want to start by thanking each of you for agreeing to be a part of this journey. We have been working together, traveling, and doing ceremony as a group for a long time. You each have put in so much of your energy to make your giveaways to the people. Your contributions are beautiful. Willow and I are so grateful."

The others in the circle took this in and shared their own sense of appreciation for the past journeys together and all the learning and growth that has occurred.

"Now let's begin to share what we have seen in these last years, leading up to the time of the new millennium, in relation to turbulence on this planet," said Willow.

"Well," began Steve, "part of my background has been in the steel industry. Being in a leadership position for some time has given me quite a broad perspective on the whole industry. Industrial output is interwoven with the automotive, aircraft, construction, and ship building concerns as well as many aspects of technology across the board. The fluctuations of employment affecting the market economy and the acceleration of technology, particularly computer technology, have created a tremendous pressure on people. I'd say many people feel driven by this pressure and what it takes to survive. Having some distance from that experience, I look back and wonder what was I doing, and where did those years go? I really wasn't living a life of choice. I found my life was being run by outside forces that I was barely conscious of. Early morning to late night, including weekends, my thoughts were filled with this pressure."

"I thank you, Steve, for your clear articulation," said Bran. "My experiences were similar, but in a different environment. I held a high-level executive position in a manufacturing company, a distillery. I experienced the same pressure you describe, and there is another level that I think many people experience. I know I did. The more I engaged in the pressure and tried to meet the expectations of my job, the more narrow my field became. I spent less time with my children and my wife. I lost touch with friends I used to spend time with. I completely abandoned any kind of physical exercise, and I began to increase my consumption of alcohol to cope with it all. Slowly, over time, there was very little meaning in what I was doing. My descriptions may sound extreme, but I've talked to many people and they seem to reflect back to me the same or very similar issues about the increased difficulty of how to find meaning in such a high-pressure life."

The group considered his words for a few minutes, and then Diane spoke. "I'd like to add something. In speaking about turbulence, I'm thinking more deeply about the inner landscape of each human. We are affected by many things around us, and what you have both been illuminating for me are the deeper aspects of cause and effect. Example: Too much acceleration equals pressure. So with this realization I can go deeper with my own reflections. I guess we all want stability and calm, yet from my river-rafting days I know everyone in the raft would go to sleep if the river was always calm. Just like too much calm, we cannot help but suffer in very serious ways when we experience too much or sustained turbulence. Therefore, I want to explore the layering, or compounding turbulence, that humans are experiencing. Take humans who have the kind of pressure you have both described. Now, add fear of loss of employment due to a fluctuating market economy. Then, add a crisis of terrorism, like we had in 2001 in New York City and Washington, D.C. And now, add the effects of war. These kinds of turbulence can create a climate of fear and insecurity."

"Thank you, Diane," said Kurt, "for your strong words and images. Now let's expand beyond the Western world's experience. There are many people in the world who have existed under a steady barrage of exaggerated turbulence for a very long time. Look at those who daily face starvation, lack of sanitation, and many kinds of deprivation. This runs all the way from a lack of clean water, to losing their homes, to wars in which their families and societies are decimated. Many live in a world of terror and injustice, having no rights or choices, where the basic freedoms we take for granted are unheard of. This overwhelming turbulence is something that most of us in the Western part of the world have never experienced. It even seems unreal to us. Many humans end up feeling powerless under these conditions. Some will turn away in fear and try to hide or escape. Unfortunately many have no way of escape. This is hard to look at, but we must if we want to really see the truth of our present reality."

For the first time there was a considerable pause in the group's exploration. Kurt had spoken what they all had seen and known, yet having it impressed on them, close up, was shocking. After a few minutes, Katherine spoke again.

"Let me take us into the next turn," Katherine said. "What I am seeing is that there comes a point in all of this turbulence, as we are calling it, when something deeper begins to emerge. Let me explain what I mean. If you look at an individual who has a tremendous amount of stress or pressure, they do their best to cope as long as they can. Then two things can happen. People may begin to experience the stress physically or emotionally, therefore staying affected by it and potentially becoming ill. Or, they will change it. The experience of this kind of stress or pressure can feel like having something you are afraid of chasing you. When you are running in fear you are simply being affected. But something altogether new happens when you stop running, face the situation, and ask yourself, 'What can I do about it?' Many feel a lot of dissatisfaction with the world. And now we are coming to the point of asking 'What can we do about it?'

"The shift we are talking about is going to come to a critical mass when many many people are ready to stand up and ask 'What is happening to our planet and what can we do to change it?' I'm not talking simply about individuals who want to help change things in their own neighborhood. I am talking about people all over the planet beginning to see things through a new lens. In this shift we are experiencing, the lens is one of interrelationship. We truly will begin to realize our interdependency and start to turn a lot of individual actions into group actions. And that will bring groups together with other groups. It is a time for moving to the power of the collective."

"Katherine, you have taken us into the next turn, as you have said. I am deeply touched by your words and images and those of the whole circle," Falcon said. "This is a powerful time, and I feel the spirits are here with us."

"Let's take some time to have a bit of fruit and tea and be with the land," said Willow. "We have opened a lot in this round. Let's absorb and come back together after some rest and reflection. When we return, let's be ready to open the discussion on what we see is beginning to emerge from this time and what attitudes are beginning to shift. Katherine, you have started us off in that direction. Let's return in an hour and a half."

Nods and murmurs of agreement moved around the circle. Little conversation was had, as each felt deeply impacted by what the others revealed. One by one they left the fire to walk or rest.

It was Falcon's turn to be fire keeper, so he stayed and looked deeply into the center of the fire. He felt a quiet stillness inside himself and a deep peace. He added wood to the fire and smoked his pipe. As he looked around he noticed the yellow-green birch leaves shimmering in the soft breeze. It was a moment that he would not forget, a moment in which he felt at one with all of life.

Falcon welcomed each of the group back around the sacred fire. They greeted each other as old friends do, with a loving touch, a nod, a look, a smile. Words were not needed among them as they were in a special ceremony of reflection and contemplation. They felt deeply connected with each other and with the power of the land they were on.

Willow pulled a small bundle from her medicine bag and slowly unwrapped it. "I'd like to use a new talking stick in this round as it seems so appropriate to this time and this ceremony. Falcon and I found this when we were in Mexico. I haven't had time to bead it yet, however the wood and the simple carving is very beautiful as it is. The lizard carved here on the end of the stick holds the dreamer medicine, and these openings symbolize the flowing of our collective potential. Let's bless it by using it for this round."

Willow closed her eyes as she held the talking stick. She felt a vibrational energy. Although she couldn't hear it, the energy was like drumming and chanting. It was coming from a long distance away, as if from another time. She opened her eyes, took a deep breath and spoke again.

"In my minds eye, I see a vibrant spider plant. Its leaves are green and white striped, lifting and leaning out from the pot in which it grows, like a community of arms outstretched to the sun. And off to one side there is a long shoot that extends way beyond the leaves and hangs down. From there begins another community of arms reaching out. I see the circles of the Earth Wisdom Way like this plant. The leaves represent the people who come together in their community to learn the old ways of wisdom, which they take into their lives, to their families and their communities. These shoots go out and start another flowering of the plant, symbolizing the ongoing natural growth of circles. When the mother plant is full of vitality it will send out many shoots of new growth.

"This image describes what has happened in our journey as teachers and message carriers. Our work has grown very organically. We have a ceremonial teaching or gathering and one person from that experience asks us to create another, and one person from that next ceremony invites us to do another. And so it goes. What I appreciate is that we receive the benefits of something growing or starting because there is a desire for it to be so. We are not pushing, therefore there is no resistance. As to what I see in this time, this story of growth and interest is accelerating. It is a time of opening. I have spoken."

Sounds of "ho" were heard as each expressed having heard and appreciated what had been painted so vividly by the images Willow shared. Bran sat to the left of Willow in the circle around the fire, and as the talking stick always travels sunwise in respect to the cycles, he was next to speak.

"I am Bran, and I am filled with the beauty of this forest of birches. I have known them to be dreamer trees in my medicine journey, and I have been noticing the way the leaves seem to shimmer in the breeze. It's a bit like I feel inside right now. I am beginning to see a wider spectrum of this journey we are on, after being with the Dreamer Chiefs in the Kiva and now reflecting on the time we are living in. I am beginning to open to the deeper significance of our being here.

"As I look at this time as a new cycle, I see a lot of movement and many early signs of a shift. I am speaking of the many circles that are forming in the United States, in the United Kingdom, and the growth of wisdom circles in Europe. We have been teaching in Germany for some time now, and like the spider plant that you spoke of, Willow, the shoots have now expanded to Austria and Denmark. We're getting requests from France, Spain, New Zealand, and even Russia. Not only are more people interested in really learning the old wisdom ways for themselves, they also see they can carry these seeds into their companies and communities.

"This last part is the most important to me, and it speaks most profoundly of the shift we are describing. People are meeting to learn and deepen in self-knowledge and remembering the old earth wisdom ways in order to assist their communities. This is the essence of interrelationships that Katherine spoke of earlier. I have spoken," said Bran.

"Ho, I am Katherine. I am appreciative of the words and images that are being spoken. After being with the Dreamer Chiefs I am experiencing something changing in myself, or maybe more to the point, my consciousness seems to be opening and expanding. It is like a series of perceptual shifts that ripple out and affect how I see and understand everything around me, and not unimportantly my own identity. It is as if I am opening to an ancient memory, or rather a kaleidoscope of remembrance that continually informs, much like waves on the shore, how I view life. I hope I'm not too vague or convoluted as I try to put this in words. It's a bit daunting to try to express what I am experiencing. I can't help but think this is happening as a direct result of being in the Kiva and now being on this dream island. So bear with me as I take a few more steps in sharing my thoughts and perceptions.

"I am experiencing my identity in an entirely different way. I guess it is always different to know something with the brain and mind and then to have a visceral experience of it. I have always known and held that I am a spirit, which has chosen to come into life in this body at this time. As I open to this kaleidoscope of remembrance, I am beginning to experience the truest nature of my identity as spirit, not even as a spirit—just pure spirit, spirit continuing. As this consciousness unfolds, I recognize I am not separate from anything else, any of you, or this island, or these trees. I have always been and I will always be. I'd say I've known this, believed this, but never had the experience of it before. This kind of understanding, or consciousness, is leading us toward the collective consciousness. Maybe it's been said already, but as we—and I mean humanity now—can approach this understanding of our true identity, we will make different decisions and take different actions.

"I took the long way around to say it, but I feel this is something that has started and is moving us forward into this shift. I have spoken."

Just then the wind lifted some fallen leaves in a small inverted cave, like a whirlwind. It danced in a complete circle around the fire and then disappeared. Each of the eight were momentarily stunned by this wind magic and belatedly said "ho" upon hearing Katherine's words of completion.

Kurt was sitting to Katherine's left and took the talking stick into his hands. Before he spoke he took time to offer wood to the fire. He also offered some tobacco, with a silent prayer. Some of the others readjusted themselves and then settled back in readiness.

"I am Kurt. Those are good words, Katherine. I guess the wind thought so, too," he said with a little smile. "I want to speak about energy and the exchange of energy. I've been studying the flow of energy for a long time, first in my business life, as a banker and investment broker, and then in these last several years in the medicine way.

"What I have come to see is that we are living in an ocean of energy, say an energy consciousness. In this ocean, there is a constant give and take where we each are in relationship with all of the energies in the universe. As humans now, we are mostly unaware of this relationship. But the old ones were masters of this understanding and knew the value of holding a high level awareness of energy exchange. It was the way they lived. For example, there was always some form of ceremonial appreciation when the hunter made a kill. Prayers and gratitude were offered for the animal's giveaway.

"Earlier in our discussion, when we spoke of the inner landscape of the human, it triggered in me an image of the human as a flowering tree. I've been holding this image, and this is what I have begun to put together.

"The more we expand our consciousness and awareness, the more we are able to create equilibrium in the inner landscape of the self. And the more conscious we are, the more choices we can make about how we respond to life as well as how we contribute to life. So, in other words, conscious humans use their energy to affect the world around them. Then, going back to the flowering tree, each of us has the opportunity, especially as we grow and expand our consciousness, to choose how we want to flower and affect the world around us.

"The instructions of the old wisdom culture were to strive to walk the path of the human, which was considered to be a high path, and to contribute to the whole by making your giveaway; in other words, to positively affect the world with your unique contribution. After all, you were a part of the community or society. It was common knowledge that all skills and abilities were needed for the whole to survive.

"So, as I look for islands of awareness in this time of turbulence I see some signs that are promising and have to do with energy exchange in the business community. First of all, I have seen one automotive industry in Germany, which has international business, bring its senior management together for four days to open the understanding of balance, first within the self, then the team, and then the whole organization. And I am in touch with a recent trend, small now, but definitely growing, which is about business taking social responsibility and business as a sustainable enterprise. This means recognizing that the actions taken by an organization affect the whole of life. Naturally this is a big step for businesses that have held that the bottom line or profit margins are their only measures of success. It is a real sign of changing attitudes when profit is no longer the only, or the prime, motivation.

"The last sign, which is possibly one of the most promising, is the growing number of organizations that are open to training their employees to use the old wisdom ways in their day-to-day operations for problem analysis and decision making. Some call it employing 'ancient technology.' This activity can be compared to a single organism, which is expanding its consciousness and consequently becomes more able to give its unique contribution and positively affect the community in which it lives. I have spoken."

"Ho" was heard around the circle.

Eva reached for the talking stick and suggested that they take some time for walking and renewing their energies. Early evening had come already, and they were approaching their second night on the island. She offered to have tea prepared upon their return, and Steve said he would prepare some berries for their evening gathering. It was Steve's time to care for the fire. He added wood and tobacco and began a song of appreciation for this time, for the spirits of the ancestors, and for the Earth Mother.

As the first stars became visible in the velvet black of the night sky, the drum called them back to the fire. Eva began.

"I want to share a dream I had last night. I was on this island, in a circle of birch trees. They were situated perfectly to represent a council circle. A fire burned in the middle, and while I stood alone at the fire, crows began to surround me. There were so many I couldn't count them all. Then one landed close to me and turned into a woman who was also still a crow. It's kind of hard to describe. She spoke one phrase—Call Council. That is what I remember.

"So today I have been looking through the dream into what is happening now and what the signs are. I know that the old councils of the people were at the heart center of their ability to live successfully as a society of people. And the way of listening deeply and in respect to each other was one aspect of it, but also the people were listening to the Sacred Source or Great Spirit. So I have been looking to see what signs of council I can find. Maybe this is some kind of clue. I assume this dream didn't come by accident.

"An event happened in Germany that I am aware of, and it has some relationship to this idea of council. A group of people I know in Munich gathered together. They didn't have a name, and they weren't a formal group. They were simply a group of friends. After the terrorist attack in New York City and Washington on the 11th of September, back in 2001, they began to get together, every night in fact, for several nights. They usually met until two or three in the morning. They were probing, questioning, looking at what happened from all angles and asking 'What can we do?'

"After some nights of these meetings, they took an action. They organized an event right in the heart of Munich, in the Marienplatz. One evening they set out a long table—60 meters long—and invited the public to come. Their purpose was to call the people together and to hear what people thought about this tragedy—just to talk together. Three hundred people came to the table! I was astonished with this outcome, especially since they weren't an existing formal group. They were simply people who cared enough to call council.

"Many of the old earth cultures, all over the planet, sat in council to gather the wisdom of the elders when they needed to understand issues they were facing and make important decisions. They would sit for two or three days and nights, with their pipes. They would listen deeply, and as they considered the issues they would speak not from any personal perspective, but from a perspective that was for the benefit of all.

"I feel deeply that humans on this planet must reawaken their council roots, and I'm encouraged because many other examples of circles and gatherings are occurring. Maybe this is the beginning of a reawakening. I will imagine it is so. I have spoken."

"Ho" was murmured softly around the circle. Right about then the soft breeze stilled, and they heard the sound of wings flapping. In the hushed silence that followed each of them looked around, but no one was able to locate the source of the sound. Eva stood to put more wood on the fire and offered her silent prayers with tobacco.

Willow was standing opposite Eva at the fire. Her stance was taut, and there was an electric quality to her energy. It was not idle curiosity that prompted the question she asked.

"Eva, before you pass on the talking stick will you describe the Crow Woman of your dream? What did she look like?"

"She was definitely a woman, while at the same time she was a crow," Eva said. "Her eyes were dark and set back in her face. Her gaze was very intense. She had a large wingspan across her shoulders with blue-black feathers. The head and back of the crow part of her was enveloping the top of her forehead almost like a headdress. Only it was very much alive. Her clothing resembled a long cape made of black shimmering feathers, which hung to the ground. Her dress, underneath, was copper colored, with patterns of shiny black beads. Does that give you a clear image?" Eva asked as she looked over at Willow.

Willow had a knowing gleam in her eyes and a small smile on her face as she thanked Eva. Willow's heart beat, then began to race, and goose bumps rose on her arms and legs as she sat down in the circle. This, Willow recognized, was not an ordinary dream. Two nights ago Willow had been visited by Crow Woman in her dream. She now felt sure this was one of their ancestors, Flys Crow, a powerful healer and leader in ancient times. Crow medicine is one that calls council. Willow knew this was a powerful message for them all. She made a strong effort to calm the excitement she was feeling and to give full attention to Steve as he began to speak.

"I am Steve," he spoke with a quiet dignity, "and I begin by singing my song of appreciation."

Each one closed their eyes and listened deeply as he sang to the ancestors.

"Thank you," he said, as he completed his chant. "I find it is necessary every now and then to bring the ancestor consciousness closer and to communicate with them directly, as we did in the Kiva. Since our journey with the Dreamer Chiefs inside the Kiva, and coming here to this island, I have felt the ancestors' presence around me. It is an amazing honor to be here and experiencing this with you. Many of my thoughts parallel what I have heard from all of you.

"My own thoughts, as I search for islands of awareness—I like that phrase, Falcon, and I hear your words about council, Eva—take me to images of tribe and community. We know the earth peoples lived in tribes or clans, in community with one another. It was a great way to pool resources and to create a sustainable way of living, where all were a part of the whole. This kind of living was based on relationship and interdependency.

"In today's world, in our so-called civilizations, we have become isolated. Our life and work encourages more competition than cooperation. City dwellers mostly don't know their neighbors, and families, for the most part, don't live together. Many are lost and have no community or sense of belonging, no tradition to help shape identity. However, many humans are questioning this.

"One sign of a change in attitude is the number of eco villages that are appearing. They are sprouting all over France, and in Spain, Portugal, Italy, and Mexico. People who want to create community, share resources, and live in balance on the earth are creating some very exciting ways of living.

"Another shift I've seen mostly in Europe is how we educate our youth. There is renewed interest in a movement called 'Free Schools,' where the parents join with the school and their children to create an educational experience that focuses on and is driven by each child's natural curiosity and unique learning interests.

"Each of these seems to be an example of humans who are willing to explore ways of being that challenge civilization's assumptions. With our experience of traveling through great cycles in the Kiva and the sense we have of the richness of life in the tribal community, I feel that these gatherings of people are like an awakening of the old ways. They hold key pieces of what needs to emerge now—the heart seeds of yearning for harmony and living in relationship with each other and the Earth Mother. I have spoken."

Appreciation was heard around the circle for Steve's words. He rose to stoke the fire, inquired how everyone was doing, and then suggested they take time to offer prayers with the sacred pipe and to reflect on what had been seen. They all agreed, and soon the ancient rattle song could be heard above the whispering wind, and the sparks from the sacred fire could be seen rising into the night sky.

The group chose to go to their dreams then, each one experiencing a fullness from the power of their ceremony and the energies of the land. It seemed as if they had been guided this entire journey and particularly on the island. Katherine remained by the fire as she would be the keeper for the next two hours. She fed the fire and gathered her woven shawl around her shoulders. She felt she was deeply held by the birch tree forest in the quiet of the night.

The Second Day of Ceremony

Their second day on the island dawned with dramatic colors filling the morning sky. A flock of geese flew overhead, their honking echoing for miles. After morning meditation and ceremonial practices the group gathered around the fire once more. They noted that the area around the fire had been swept with branches, and greens from the pines graced the stones which surrounded Chemah, the Sacred Fire. The air of the morning was crisp and cool, sending shivers as an advance warning. Soon the winter cold would make its home on the island.

Diane stood at the fire with the talking stick in her hands. She offered tobacco to the four directions and above and below and placed it in the fire. She was a tall graceful woman with shoulder-length chestnut hair. Her brown eyes held a depth that seemed to be an inner pathway to her soul. She sat down and began.

"I am Diane. I give thanks to my ancestors and Mother Life for guiding me here in this time. My medicine path has not always been easy, and my ways of learning have been varied and at times very challenging. I can say now I am grateful for each one. I know we each choose the path we walk, consciously or unconsciously. Hopefully I am now choosing more consciously in my life.

"I feel that ocean of consciousness you described Kurt, like I am floating in it, and I am way more expanded than I have ever been. In the night I had many dreams, but none seem to have stuck in my consciousness long enough to register. The only thing I remember waking up with is a strong energy of responsibility. So I will offer my contribution looking through this lens. You will know my past journey and the kind of lessons I asked life to teach me."

Diane shifted position a bit and continued. "I think one of the biggest lessons has been about my own responsibility—responsibility for my life, for my actions, and especially for what goes on inside me in relation to outside events. It is what makes the difference in whether I see myself as a victim or not. That was a pivotal understanding that came to me most deeply through these old wisdom ways we carry. I know that the understanding of self-authority is at the heart of this old way. I remember when my first teacher taught me how self-authority really meant self-authorship and that I was in some way responsible for everything that came to me in my life. I, of course, didn't want to hear any of it. There was quite a bit I would much rather blame on someone—anyone—else. But when I finally understood that when I needed to learn something and had chosen that particular experience to learn it, my resistance faded.

"In the old ways when there was a healing that was needed for a member of the tribe, the whole community would gather to participate. After the healing all would consciously hold the person as having been healed. In this way they shared the responsibility for the outcome, as if they acted as one body.

"In training the youth within a society or clan there was a similar enactment. I remember one of the grandmothers, Ancient Rain, who shared this story with me.

"There was a young woman, she said, who had shown her temper and some very bad manners, causing embarrassment to her family and tribe. Instead of punishing her, they called council with her, the woman she had offended, and all other women in the society of women. The elder grandmother spoke first, apologizing to the other woman and to this young woman for not being a better example and for not teaching her effectively enough how to conduct herself as a young woman.

"The next person to speak was the next oldest. She spoke and said she took responsibility for this sad event and offered her apology as well. It went on, each in turn. Each woman spoke her apology and took her responsibility for not being a better teacher or a better guide or a better sister. The young woman underwent an amazing transformation as she learned how to take responsibility for herself and her own actions. This was the story Ancient Rain told.

"It seems, in my experience, that being seen in a community and having that community act as a mirror is a transformational gift and one most rare in our present society. However, I have seen a trend that is gaining momentum, due to the real healing that takes place. It is called *restorative justice,* and it parallels some of the old wisdom ways. When a crime is committed in a community, rather than the person going through the traditional justice system, ending in punishment or fine, all the people that have been affected are called together. They come together in one room, often sitting in a circle, and tell their stories of what happened and how they were impacted. The offending person also tells what they did, why he or she did what they did, and shares their feelings. By telling their stories the truth from their hearts emerges, and healing begins.

"This has elements of our tribal beginnings and allows the responsibility for actions to be owned and shared by all in the community. The one who has committed the action is also held by the community so genuine restoration occurs.

"I also see this as an example of a shift in consciousness. When the people tell their stories this way we all become listeners as well as storytellers. A special magic happens in the telling, as we become aware of some of the hidden layers within ourselves. In the restorative justice process we may begin with enmity, but our stories create bridges of understanding and forgiveness. These are important elements which can lead us towards a culture of higher consciousness. I have spoken."

Appreciative murmurs of "ho" were heard around the circle. Each of them breathed deeply of the cool autumn air and resettled themselves while Diane added wood and tobacco to the fire. All waited expectantly for Falcon to begin. Soon he rose and stood at the fire for a time, offering prayers to the ancestors and offering an ancient Cheyenne love song. The song is an expression of love for the universe and everything in it. When finished, he picked up the talking stick and began.

"What do we need to see?" Falcon asked emphatically. "I have been asking myself this in these last days and in the night. I spent time at the fire with several of you, and I have had many dreams. It is vitally important that we are here. I feel this in my bones. But what are we here for? This has been my focus.

"Last night I began reviewing what events called us here and what has been revealed to us, in the Kiva time and here. You all know about Willow's dream about finding the tree—it's called Tulipan Africanis by the way—with seeds in the shape of a heart. We found the tree the first morning on our trip to the Yucatan. That was followed by my strong urge to have a pipe ceremony on the top of the pyramid in Coba. It was there that the vision and message came from the Mayan Priestess.

"These events were no accident. We feel we were called here on purpose. This is why I am taking the time to go over everything again so we can put all we are learning into perspective. So let's go into what we heard from the time at the pyramid in Coba.

"We were told in our vision that this is a time of great change. The earth is coming to completion of a 5,000 year cycle, which will open the door to a new manifestation of the human spirit. A change of consciousness will take place. It is a time of great potential. This calls for high awareness, and we have a role to play. This is an important point.

"We've experienced a journey into the past, in the Kiva through the mind of the Medicine Singers. And here on this island we have been looking at the early signs of the collective consciousness as it begins to shift.

"So, what is our role? What do we do with all we have seen? Let's hold that question as we reflect on the beginning signs. We've seen this as an opening time, where the growth of circles is accelerating and the evidence of inter-relationship is indicated as people are taking the old wisdom ways into their families, work and communities. Many businesses are moving toward social responsibility, recognizing their effect on the world and communities around them. As well, some organizations are bringing old traditional ways into their day-to-day operations. We have seen this beginning. Many are moving from hierarchal forms to flat organizations with less and less male-dominated hierarchical, military-style leadership. A return of the use of council and the eco village trend is accelerating, along with many forms of alternative communities, representing humans who are choosing to live in relation to the natural cycles of the earth. The Free School Movement is growing in Europe and non-religion-based home schooling is growing in the United States. A system of restorative justice is taking hold as individuals and communities are taking responsibility for healing together. People, in general, seem to be less willing to work so many hours that the rest of their life is put on hold. We are shifting from a becoming society to a society which may be able to balance being and becoming.

"All these signs herald the shift of consciousness that we have been sensing and preparing for. It feels to me like this is the beginning of what is to come. We have seen these things. We have been touched in these days and nights by the land and the spirits here. This has been a deeply-altering time, and yet some pieces are still missing. This is the question that remains. I have the feeling we will know what we need to know before long. I have spoken."

As Falcon was speaking his last words, the sound of Susquona's motor could be heard in the distance, announcing the approach of the Dreamer Chiefs. Each smiled in anticipation of the chiefs' arrival and waited for Willow to pick up the talking stick, as it is tradition for the person who started the round to bring it to completion.

As Willow made her offering to the sacred fire, she looked up and saw a bevy of dragonflies dancing, swooping, and careening in an acrobatic delight above them. With a smile of awe and wonder she began.

"Magic is above us, around us, and approaches us," she said as she gestured in the direction of the Dream Chiefs. "We are filled with the magic of life expressing itself. I have listened deeply to all of your words, and I thank each of you most sincerely for each of your thoughtful contributions. Each part is helping to create the image and understanding of our present condition on this planet.

"Falcon," she said, looking at him, "I appreciate the summary you made and the thoughts you have added. I share the question of 'what next?' with you. I believe we all do. I've been doing a lot of dreaming in this time, and being here on this powerful island is opening something in me as well. Every sense is heightened, and my dreams are vivid each night. I feel like I know this place, as if I have been here before. I can't explain it but I have been here. I just don't know how or when. I carry the memory of this place, and I know there is a reason that we, each of us, have been chosen to come here.

"Something has come back to me, Falcon. I remembered when you were speaking about the vision we shared in Coba. It was something the Priestess said at the very end. I had completely forgotten it until I heard you speaking just now. She said something about us being part of this journey and that we will need to see deeply into the role that we and those like us will play in the time ahead. So now I feel it is clear to me. We are being prepared for the role we need to play. We have been called here to prepare us to play a part in this great time of turning."

Just then Willow was interrupted by Susquona's call from the shore.

"I have spoken, for now" she said.

Enthusiastic sounds of "ho" were spoken as they arose and hurried to welcome Susquona and the Dreamer Chiefs.

Feasting and Challenge

The two groups greeted each other warmly and everyone helped unload the items they had brought in the boat. The shores were soon dotted with blankets, boxes, baskets, and other odd shaped parcels. While everyone was busy unloading and securing the boat, the Old Man and Old Woman laid down a blanket and set out a small feast on the rock ledge that extended out over the water. A large flat rock, it made a perfect table for bowls and cups full of moose meat and berries and containers of clear water. Stomachs rumbled as they approached. The Dreamer Chiefs invited them to sit and take part in a small feast, prepared just for them.

The Old Man spoke first of the moose meat being food of remembrance. As he spoke mouths were watering and hungry stomachs were turning over with expectation.

"The moose brought memory because it dined on the reeds that grow in and around the stones. The stones remember all and are the oldest of the children of the earth," he said. Each one felt a rush of energy as they took in this marvelous food. The moose meat had been dried in the summer camp, the Old Woman explained, and she had picked the berries that morning. There was plenty for everyone, and each found themselves challenged in how to express the unprecedented amount of enjoyment and appreciation they were experiencing.

Soon they had cleaned up what remained from the feast and began to transport the many baskets and parcels to the camp nearby. Fast work was made of setting up the tents for Susquona and the Dreamer Chiefs and storing the supplies in the small kitchen. Then, settling by the fire, each with a cup of tea, the Dreamer Chiefs asked Willow and Falcon to tell the story of the days and nights since they had last seen them.

The Old Man and the Old Woman nodded frequently and listened intently to all that was spoken. When Falcon and Willow completed the story, the Dreamer Chiefs described their own time of ceremony and how in their dreaming time they had visited this circle more than once in the last two days.

The Old Woman then stood and opened one of the many parcels held in her basket. She unwrapped a beautiful piece of soft leather, which had been fashioned with small blue and white seed beads. At the same time the Old Man stood and unwrapped another package, with a similar necklace fashioned from leather and beads. They walked to Willow and Falcon and asked them to stand.

Softly, the Old Woman began to sing while she held the necklace in the air, offering it to the four directions. She then placed the necklace on Willow. Seeing the beauty in the Old Woman's face, Willow's heart felt as if it was in her throat.

The Old Man took his time as he looked into Falcon's eyes and chanted before he placed the necklace around Falcon's neck. Willow and Falcon were asked to remain standing while more bundles were unwrapped.

The Dreamer Chiefs then walked to Bran and Katherine and presented them each with a necklace. This process was repeated with Kurt and Eva and Steve and Diane. Finally, with them all standing, the Old Man spoke.

"You stand here on sacred ground. This place has been the home of many dreamer ceremonies in the history of the people. This is where the Old Ones came to dream. You have been called here because we have some important work to do together.

"Around your neck has been placed a dreamer necklace made by the Old Woman. She has held you and prayed for you in this ceremony time. She honors you for being seed carriers of the dream."

"Prepare now for a purification lodge," said the Old Woman. "We will enter the Rainbow Lodge together when the first star shines in the night sky. We will enter the place of Mystery together. We must ready ourselves to allow the Mystery to speak to us of the message of this time."

The Dreamer Chiefs left the circle while each member of the circle stood looking into the fire, savoring this time of wonder.

Preparation of the Rainbow Lodge

The people assembled in the early afternoon to gather what was needed for the Rainbow Lodge, a particular form of the Inipi Lodge held sacred as a healing and purifying ritual. The women went with Willow to gather the birch boughs to make the lodge. They found a perfect place with a stand of birch that had the new flexible growth needed for the roundness of the structure. Offering their prayers with tobacco while singing softly to the birch tree branches, the women imaged the beauty of the Rainbow Lodge as they asked the birch to giveaway for their sacred ritual.

Falcon and Susquona spoke of the need for stones and wood for the Rainbow Lodge fire. They stood in an abundant land. All around them, wherever the eye could see, was dry wood that had been cured winter after winter, simply awaiting their need of it. Around the edge of the island were ancient stones, which had been polished smooth through the many cycles of ice, wind, rain, and sun. As the men gathered the stones and wood, each of them began their preparation for the evening ceremony. They knew what lay ahead for them. They knew that when they entered the Rainbow Lodge it was a sacred space, space where they would meet the divine source.

Singing was heard across the water as the women began to create the lodge. Their voices rose and fell in beautiful harmony as the women sung their prayers, calling the ancestors to accompany them in this sacred ritual. The birch lodge structure, with its strongly-woven dome, was then covered with many colorful blankets, gently, lovingly, as if they were dressing an honored grandmother. Each blanket was opened and offered to the four directions for blessing.

The men had readied the place for the fire, 20 paces in front of the Rainbow Lodge, and stacked the wood nearby. While the women dressed the lodge, the men began to create the Rainbow Lodge fire. As the wood and dry branches were alternately placed, each stone was set carefully. When finished it held over 50 stones and resembled an ancient pyramid. Many tobacco prayers had gone into building the small pyramid, and now it was ready to light.

The women joined the men as the sun quietly slipped below the horizon. Chanting an ancient song of appreciation, the Old Man and the Old Woman walked to the fire. The sky was filled with orange, magenta, pink, and purple, and a full moon would soon appear.

Willow and Falcon lit the fire. A soft drumming began. It was a time for silence, introspection, and prayer.

Ceremony of the Rainbow Lodge

It was dark now, and the dancing light of the fire showed shifting patterns of color on the blankets that covered the semi-spherical shape of the lodge. The setting

Chapter Eight—The Realization

was magical. In the light cast by the fire, the faces of each of the group appeared to have a timeless and ancient quality, as if they were people who belonged in this place and had been here many times in ages past.

Susquona, holding the place of firekeeper, shifted the burning logs of the fiery pyramid, revealing glimpses of the white hot stones. As he adjusted the logs, showers of brilliant sparks rose into the dark night.

Pointing with her staff at the fire, the Old Woman spoke. "We see the presence of the ancient grandmother and grandfather stones beckoning to us with their white faces from the fire of Chemah. Their presence and their wisdom will purify and open us in the Rainbow Lodge as we seek with our prayer thoughts for that which the Sacred Mystery reveals to us."

"Let us now enter this Sacred Lodge," spoke the Old Man. "We present ourselves with open hearts into this womb of the universe where the earth stones, filled now with fire, will join with the water and air to purify our thoughts and open us to what will come."

One at a time each in the group stooped to go through the doorway and enter the Rainbow Lodge. The Old Woman went in first, crawling to her space by the stone pit next to the doorway. The Old Man went second and sat next to the Old Woman. The others followed, sitting around the interior wall of the lodge, with Falcon and Willow entering last, to sit by the doorway.

"Four rounds we will have," intoned the Old Woman. "One, for the internal fire of the sun and stars. Two, for the purity of the earth body temple. Three, for the sound of the cleansing waters that flower the innocence. Four, for the breath of Wehomah, the air, which brings clarity and courage.

"We are here, sacred spirits," she sang, "to receive your healing blessing and to open to your Mystery."

The Old Woman called for Susquona to bring in eleven hot stones to the pit. The Old Man chanted and shook his deer-hoof rattle. The stone grandparents came into the lodge, one by one. The door to the lodge was then closed and the darkness of the universe surrounded the group.

First Door

    The swirling mist of hot primordial vapor
    Clears as dancing points of light move above,
    High keening sounds sing notes of memory,
    Broken by cracks of thunder,
    Voice of timeless journeys.
    Silence.
    Whispers calling to wakeful dreaming.
    We are here now,
    Be now,
    Listen now,
    Coming now,
    Burning bright now,
    We are.
    I am in the Universe.
    The door opens,
    Hot steam rising into the night sky.
    Silence.
    Opening.
    The Old Woman calls for 12 stones.

Second Door

    Ancient stones enter,
    Steaming now,
    Singing now,

Pouring out the cup of life through myriad portals,
Breathing in,
Welcoming in,
Shapes close the perimeter of darkness.
Rising up,
They form and move with almond eyes.
Strong bodied shapes
Merge and sit between the spaces,
Occupied by the dark breathing body of prayerful
Thought.
The Universe is in my body.
The doorway opens.
Expansion.
Breath.
Light.
Silence of the night.
The Old Woman calls for 13 stones.

Third Door

Stones enter,
Grandmothers, grandfathers,
Ho, welcome.
Smell of sweetgrass fills the lodge.
With resonant tone,
Space is filled with deep
Sibilant voice of sound.
Drum beat,
Moving feet and hard packed earth.
Ancient song from throats of dancers past,
Crying out the joyous return.
Sounds emerging,
The river of life flowing.

The Universe and I combine together.
Doorway opening,
Steam escapes,
Timeless,
Void.
Limitless being.
The Old Woman calls for 14 stones.

Fourth Door
Calling the old ones,
Ho, Grandmother, welcome,
Ho, Grandfather, welcome.
Steady rhythm,
Light in the darkness grows.
Breathing now,
Lungs filled with exultant cries,
New born to return,
A destiny of courage to unfold,
Dawning of new cycle,
Long awaited,
We are here once more,
We are returning now.
We are One.

The door to the Rainbow Lodge opens. Steam rises from the opened door into the night sky. From within the lodge the seekers look out toward the fire. The circle of bright red-hot coals, surrounded by the night and the ring of forest beyond, welcomes them back.

Each seeker has had the sensation of having stepped out of the flow of time, and yet the stars above have only traveled a quarter of their arc across the night sky. Deep in the altered state of silence, the night cry of the loon calls them to be present once again. All in the lodge are profoundly affected.

The swishing sound of the Old Woman's rattle begins as she speaks. "Oh Sacred Mother, we have called and we have heard and seen. We are renewed and leave this womb born anew."

Stepping forth from the Rainbow Lodge entrance, each raises their arms to the starlit sky in a prayer of gratitude. All gather in a circle, seated around the bright warmth of the ember mound. As they gaze into the coals of burning wood, Susquona places robes around the shoulders of each silent figure.

Willow's Prayer

After a time, Willow rises and speaks slowly and deliberately. Speaking aloud a prayer that has built inside her in this time, she sends it out into the universe.

"I am Willow. There are some words I want to speak. Tonight I address the collective consciousness of all humans that are living, have lived, and will live.

"There is much on this journey that has been revealed, and tonight I speak simply as a voice of spirit expressing itself. Some would say it is foolish to speak this way in the dark of the night, with none to listen but the stars and a few dreaming lizards. I know however that our thoughts can travel across this planet, and in this way I send them out as a prayer.

"I speak tonight to all who dream of a world that is kind, to all who dream of a warm safe place to live and to care for their children, with enough to eat and a clean place in which to grow.

"I call out to you tonight. I reach out to you with my heart and with my hand. Don't be afraid to dream. Our dreams of a different way can come true. Believe in this. Believe with me.

"We can't change things alone. Only together we can. Come to stand with me. Whisper your dream into the night. Sing your song to the stars. They are listening. We are listening.

"My song is one of hope, hope that we will truly listen to what we know inside. We know how to listen. We know how to be forgiving. We know how to understand. We can take the first step toward the kind of world we want.

"I know some carry old pain and fear and anger. And still I ask, can we remember a time before that?

"The old ones knew how to remember the essence of our true identity. That essence is love. Let us remember. Together. We can. We must."

Recognition and Relevation

The brilliant stroke of a meteor's path blazes across the dark, followed by the soft movement of the wind through the trees. It is like a gentle urging to look at one another, and as we do our eyes shine with the awe of remembrance. In the flickering glow from the embers, we see our visages are shifting, the familiar faces changing to ancient elders and back again. Eagle-plumed headdresses and beaded tunics of white deerskin alternate in the shifting light with damp tousled hair atop the shining clear faces of the dear ones we know.

We have all begun a transformation of consciousness. Recognition comes to us as a collective inspiration. We are a part of those returning.

In this moment of illumination the consciousness of each of us is flooded with the remembrance of our previous journey here, as elders and chieftains. Each of us remembers that journey of a different time, when we were in the cave beneath the waters. We remember the time and seeing what would be needed when we returned.

Now, in this moment, sitting around the coals of the Rainbow Lodge fire, each of us experiences being both one of the old ancestors and the present self, who we are in this cycle.

the Future

Speaking to the spirits in the night.
It is a practice held long.
Telling the dreams of the heart
Is like a melody.
Each one,
Floating into the cool night air.
When they find each other,
There is beauty.

Nagawah, North Giver (2003)

part Four
A New Era

CHAPTER NINE
Parting the Veil

Given the remembrance and the revelation that the consciousness of the ancient people is part of the reality of who they are, the small band that came to the Dreamer Island have returned to the world and shared their remembrance of the ancient chiefs' council in many places around the planet.

After saying farewell to the Dreamer Chiefs, Willow and Falcon and their companions spent several weeks absorbing the impact of the revelation they had experienced together. During this time they formulated a plan of sharing their new awareness with others around the world. Through many associations doors were opened to allow different members of the group to make presentations to large audiences in major centers around the world. The presentations were well received by the many people who attended, and many stepped forward wanting to play a part in the furthering of this consciousness to bring forth a new era for humanity.

A Year Later—The Vision

A year has passed, 365 turnings of the Mother Earth, and the band of seekers has returned to the Dreamer Isle. They are accompanied by large numbers of those who have been touched by the information and images of the ancient chiefs' council.

To be able to take the needed actions that the ancient chiefs have recommended, the large band has determined they must visit the cave of the obsidian mirror. There they will enter into the future. By seeing this future they will be informed of the steps they need to take as they create the new era.

There are multitudes of us now, from all lands of the Mother Earth, gathered here in this place. Men, women and children of all colors and ages, we gaze upward at the beauty of the night sky.

Suddenly the stars begin to turn at a blurring speed. It is as if the earth we are standing on is spinning faster and our reference points for time and space are shifting dramatically. There is no crying or sounds of terror amongst us. There is only a profound silence of awe and wonder at our awakening.

The change has come, and those of us here see one another in a treasured moment of recognition. We have returned, as old and new, and with this realization the night sky resumes its measured pace of celestial beauty, but with a new brilliance, as if a veil has been sloughed off.

There is magic in the air.

The breath we take in is alive with an invigorating sweet perfume, filling each of us with hope. The vast number who have gathered here are touched by this experience of remembrance. With one flow of thought we now know this is the time of the heart seeds' opening. We quickly understand it is time for us to look into our future together in the dreaming way of the old chiefs.

Looking Seven Generations Ahead

Many fires are created in stone circles around the island by the throng of people who have assembled here and gathered around each fire circle. The people sit comfortably to prepare for their dreaming journey, returning to the cave of the obsidian mirror.

As the dreaming state comes to the people, they descend into the watery depth together and travel in dreamtime to the sun-striped beach before the cave's entrance.

Entering, we all descend into the open dome of the cave and sit before the black obsidian mirror once more. We see with one mind. We are many. We have returned. We know the time the women chiefs had foreseen is now.

The Old Dreamers knew they carried a vital responsibility, through their dreams, for what was created in the future. They knew their ability to form images through thought would create form. When they used this power intentionally, it was like a message sent out to the universe, like a deep prayer.

The Dreamers were taught to follow that prayer thought with their gratitude as they knew their prayer was heard and would be answered. All they needed to do was to walk toward that future and continue to hold the image in their minds' eyes.

Calling upon that which we have been and that which we are now, we open our vision in the tradition of the dreamers. We see into the future, the future that we call into being, like a prayer.

Passing through the leaves of imagery of seven generations the visions in the obsidian mirror reveal a time some 150 years in the future. We see this time together, with one mind, one awareness, one consciousness.

Opening The Dream of The Future

The transformation wrought by the impact of an evolving higher consciousness is visible in the multitude of diverse forms of human social manifestation. But a common form underlies all the populations of people on the Mother Earth. This common form is known as clustering, and it has taken the place of city and metropolis gatherings characteristic of past eras.

This form of social organization is a natural and organic gathering of humans in groups of 20 to 40 families of approximately 320 men, women, and children, living in geographical neighborhoods in proximity with common needs and ties of relationship.

In these ecologically-balanced geographical areas, humans have formed clusters of up to 100 or so of these family groups. They self-govern, by councils, and provide an economic base for food, shelter, tools, and clothing that is in harmony with the local bioregion the clusters occupy.

Technology and the ancient wisdom ways have combined into a higher form, providing for human needs in a way known as *harthotology* (har-thot'-ol-ogy). Harthotology is founded on a marriage of heart wisdom and imaginative thought discipline. This way of human behavior has evolved from the revolutionary effects of an evolving higher consciousness, which has permeated the human presence on the Mother Earth.

In this vision, seven generations in the future, it is seen by those looking into the obsidian mirror that the human population has stabilized at approximately four billion. This has resulted from a universally-agreed on program among clusters to limit family sizes. These four billion humans now reside in self-regulating clusters. These clusters are connected and related by representation using the techniques of harthotology of the higher consciousness.

Education of young and old is universal and integrated with this new and purer organic science of heart, mind, and thought. Disease and imbalance, both in humans and in the other life forms on the Mother Planet, has been largely replaced by the natural health and well-being of humans, plant life, and animals. Many species of animals flourish in vast reserves of free-space, shared-space, and park lands all around the Mother Earth.

Each cluster community supports and participates in a council of eight areas of focus. There is rich cultural diversity around the world, and some of the characteristics of these self-organizing communities come before us in the imagery of the obsidian mirror.

People living in these groups have time and enthusiasm to self-govern in wisdom councils. They hold and care for shared values, such as living well with shared effort, creating sustainable methods of livelihood, teaching and caring for the young, and fostering significant roles for elders, which utilizes the resource of their experience.

We see that religious and spiritual practices in the clusters have much diversity and freedom, and there is cross sharing in times of celebrations and community gatherings. In the lifestyle of the cluster communities, all the family groups contribute to a rich variety of celebrations and seasonal ceremonies where the arts and crafts skills of the people are displayed, utilized, and traded.

All the families contribute so members can travel and rotate living time between clusters. This nourishes connections and relationships.

We see many new educational models where students and parents are choosing where and how they learn. The educational system includes curriculum on ways of healing, principles of peace, self-knowledge, and how to live in harmony with the planet.

In the business of providing needed goods, materials, and services, geographical combinations of clusters and their resources are organized within a 100-mile radius. In these areas, entrepreneurs and cooperative enterprises work together, guided by community needs and regulated by the areas' representative councils. Creativity and innovation incorporate principles of sustainability and resource restoration.

Women and men share equal roles and functions in leadership and in the work force. Work efforts are accomplished by rotating teams where the individual average work week is 20 hours, and another ten hours is devoted to community services and the arts.

We see in this time that sustaining a new era of health and well-being for every individual is a world-wide focus, and this is a primary focus in cluster communities everywhere. Average life expectancy of the human has exceeded the 100-year span. This is due to the adoption of higher consciousness health practices, which promote balance and vigor of well-being in the realms of spirit, body, emotions, and mind.

Cluster communities provide quarterly retreats for all members to balance and restore their health in these four areas. They practice meditation, exercise, play, and participate in guided vision quests and other forms of cleansing and renewal.

Western medicine has been largely replaced by natural-earth medicine practices that draw on the body's own intelligence to nurture the whole organism's natural functioning. Trained health practitioners are members of every cluster community's service group. This focus is one of the primary elements in fostering the discipline of peace throughout the world.

World relations have reached a high level of harmony and connectedness in all areas. Humans flourish due to amazing communications development processes. These communication processes enable the energies of physical matter to appear in distant areas in holographic form. Because this capacity of communication is available to everyone, the walls of separation and isolation, which fostered divisiveness and lack of understanding in the past, have fallen away. Old patterns of strife and conflict in areas of nationalism and religion have been supplanted by direct communications, using these new processes, between the geographical clusters' councils, as well as between individuals.

Amongst the many groups that are present in the dreaming cave, a rich tapestry of images flow like rivers from the vision that has been seen. The minds and hearts of the dreamers are filled with awe and joy as this dreaming time comes to a close.

Reflections on the Dreamtime

As the people awaken from the dreaming time, they all gather in a large clearing on the island to listen to the Dreamer Chiefs. The Old Woman begins.

"Collectively we have stepped into the obsidian mirror to view a transformed and healed era. We see that the human species has come of age. We humans no longer think and act like adolescents, considering only ourselves.

We have become more concerned and attentive to the well-being of our planet earth and have come to see we are indeed interdependent, in the most positive sense."

The Old Man continues. "As humans we have realized it takes each of us to hold this world in a balanced way. We have finally understood that diversity of perspective does not need to create conflict. Rather, a wholeness of perspective, incorporating multiple views, leads us to a deeper understanding of our challenges and helps us create better solutions.

"The journey into the obsidian mirror has revealed our dreams. We have spoken what we want to create, the dreams that are residing in our hearts. They are the seeds we have planted into the collective consciousness. Now they have taken root."

Each of the people who have shared the future dream recognize that they, along with all others who carry the heart seeds of the dream, must stand and speak of what is possible. All of them feel they must carry the message of hope in their lives and into the world.

There is one final night to sleep and dream on the island. Small fires all over the island punctuate the dark of the night as the people reflect on the magic revealed in the dreamtime. Amazement, delight, and anticipation are felt as the people prepare for sleep. Along with anticipating the future are questions in the consciousness of the people: How can I help? What can I do? How will we get to this dream of the future?

As the new moon makes herself visible most of the fires have become embers and the people have entered the night dream. There in the night dream, the questions the people have been asking open the door to a collective dream that they all share.

The Animal Council

In the shared dream all of the people are gathered in a very large clearing in a great forest of ancient trees. A drum is sounding the slow rhythm of the heart beat of the Mother Earth.

An animal council has been called. There are representatives from every part of the animal kingdom. The insect people have traveled for over a year to arrive on time for this council. They will hold the Northwest and Northeast perspectives. The flying people have been able to travel more swiftly and are represented by Eagle who will hold the perspective of the East.

There are those who swim and those who travel on four legs, small and large, beautiful and peculiar. They have all gathered, somehow knowing the questions that would be asked by the humans.

In the dream the people see themselves gathered all around the animals. There is a hush as Crow begins to speak.

"We have come in answer to your call. You have asked us questions that reside in your heart of sincerity, and we have come to speak with you in council. Listen well, human friends. We have come in respect for the dreams you hold of a new era of healing and transformation. We speak to each of you directly."

Eagle, from the realm of spirit, speaks first, from the East.

"As you seek your role in the creation of the new era, remember to give your soul wings of freedom to fly high each day so that you can express the beauty of your spirit," said Eagle. "The beauty of your spirit is your gift to life. Find your own way to come in touch with your sacredness and the sacredness of life. Do it every day."

Next Jaguar, eyes of the night, steps forward to speak from the perspective of the Southeast.

"Remember you have been given the senses which allow you to be aware of the experience within yourself and all around you. Take time to be still and present with your experience," said Jaguar. "Fill your heart and mind with true appreciation for your life. Keep your heart open for understanding, especially when it is most difficult."

Badger, fierce defender, speaks from the South.

"Be fierce and alert in caring for the innocence and trust within yourself and those around you. Avoid the danger of unspoken conflict, which can divide and isolate. Do not let your emotions rule you. Use them to listen to the deeper parts of yourself, and then choose how you want to respond," said Badger.

Wolf, the keeper of memory, speaks next, from the Southwest.

"You are each a traveler of the sacred path. You come from a long line of travelers before you. Be simple in your dedication of purpose, so that others may follow. Your life, your learning, and your experience has shaped who you are. Come to deeply know your own journey. Awaken your dream of yourself. Trust you are on your way."

Bear, the winter dreamer, speaks from the West.

"Seek balance in all your thoughts, words, and actions to bring harmony and caring for your people," said Bear. "Remember you have the ability to heal yourself and others around you. Begin by respecting yourself and listening to your deepest wisdom. Then expand this to others in your life."

Spider, the weaver of the web of life, speaks from the Northwest.

"Delicate are the strands that weave the web of relationship. Be mindful of the cycles and rhythms of all of nature as you move to create a new era. Do not use force in an untimely fashion, but let the flow of the sacred winds and tides carry the strands of higher consciousness to form your connections," reminded Spider quietly.

"See your own journey in this life as one of learning. You are an important part of the web of life. What you think, say, and do affects everything. Be aware of and responsible for yourself."

Buffalo, keeper of the giveaway, speaks from the North perspective.

"Within you is limitless resource, both for yourself and for the people. Wisdom is your heritage. You can draw upon the strength of your knowing heart and bring clarity to your next step. Your heart is the deepest part of you and knows what is right. Speak the truth of your heart. Stand for what is important," Buffalo emphasized with a stamp of her hoof.

Dragonfly, messenger of magic, speaks from the last perspective of the council, the Northeast.

"Take these words of our council into yourself and form and reform them into the magical sword of your own integrity. You are a magical being. You are pure potential. You can change your life. You have the power to change the world." With a great fluttering of wings Dragonfly paused and asked, "What role do you choose to play?"

In the depth of the night the stars shine down on the sleeping multitudes, while the dream images of the council of animals and their words of wisdom meld into the human's deep consciousness.

A new dawn is coming.

www.ingramcontent.com/pod-product-compliance
Lightning Source LLC
Chambersburg PA
CBHW071810080526
44589CB00012B/738